Advance Praise for *Passport to Freedom*

"Nizam Missaghi's gripping memoir is a testament to the indomitable human spirit and the pursuit of freedom against all odds. His story of courage, resilience, and the unwavering determination to reclaim his future is both harrowing and inspiring. Missaghi's words capture not just the peril of his escape from the Islamic Republic but the profound cost of living without liberty."

—Borzou Arjmand, award-winning Iranian actor, producer, playwright, musician, and activist

"As an actor who has faced discrimination firsthand, I found *Passport to Freedom* to be a deeply personal and powerful journey that echoes the struggles of generations who have dared to dream beyond imposed limitations. This book is not just a story—it's a lifeline for anyone who has ever been told they cannot, reminding us that freedom is always worth the fight."

—Shabnam Tolouei, award-winning actor, director, and filmmaker

"A spirited testimony to the American Dream, *Passport to Freedom* is a captivating story of escape and homecoming."

—Donia Bijan, author of *Maman's Homesick Pie* and *The Last Days of Café Leila*

PASSPORT TO FREEDOM

FROM TEHRAN *to* TRIUMPH

NIZAM MISSAGHI, M.D.

A REGALO PRESS BOOK
ISBN: 979-8-89565-473-6
ISBN (eBook): 979-8-89565-474-3

Passport to Freedom:
From Tehran to Triumph

Cover Design by Conroy Accord

Publishing Team:
Founder and Publisher – Gretchen Young
Managing Editor – Caitlin Burdette
Production Manager – Kate Harris
Production Editor – Rachel Paul

As part of the mission of Regalo Press, a donation is being made to The Simpatico Foundation Inc., as chosen by the author. Find out more about this organization at https://thesimpatico.org/.

Regalo Press
New York • Nashville
regalopress.com

Published in the United States of America
1 2 3 4 5 6 7 8 9 10

This book is first and foremost dedicated to my late mother, Dr. Tahereh Berjis—my role model, my guiding light, and the very reason I chose the path of medicine. Her commitment to social responsibility, education, and women's issues made her a woman ahead of her time. Through her compassion, strength, and unwavering commitment to healing and service, she taught me that medicine is not merely a profession, but a lifelong calling—one that carries forward across generations. Her life continues to inspire everything I strive to be.

I also dedicate this book to my father, Ziaollah Missaghi, whose wisdom, insight, and remarkable problem-solving mind have always lifted me higher. His thoughtful guidance and steady support have shaped my journey in ways beyond measure.

And finally, this book is dedicated to my children—Darian, Kamdin, and Aran—my greatest source of hope for the future. You were born into a free world, one made possible by the sacrifices of those who came before you. My wish is that you always cherish that freedom, understand its value, and honor the struggles that secured it. May the world you inherit feel vast with opportunity, compassion, and purpose.

To each of you—my parents, my sister, and my children—I offer my deepest love and gratitude. You enrich my life, the life of our family, and your community in countless ways. This work is as much yours as it is mine.

FOREWORD

There are moments when you encounter a story that does more than inform and entertain you. It stretches your sense of what is possible and how the human spirit can both endure and transform. *Passport to Freedom* is one of those rare stories.

In my work—both as an actor and as someone deeply curious about spirituality, humanity, and the forces that shape our collective consciousness—I've had the privilege of meeting people from every conceivable background. Through conversations sparked by my podcast Soul Boom and beyond, I've listened to voices of wisdom born from comfort and, just as often, wisdom forged in adversity.

What has become increasingly clear to me is a simple yet profound truth: when individuals are denied opportunity by circumstance, oppression, or injustice—and are forced to leave their homeland in search of freedom—something extraordinary happens.

Yes, the individuals who escape repression benefit from the open air of liberty. They finally get to breathe. They finally get to learn, to create, to heal, to build. But just as importantly, the societies that receive them are enriched beyond measure. There is a mutuality here. A synergy. A kind of spiritual and intellectual exchange that elevates everyone involved.

History proves it again and again. Refugees and immigrants who arrive carrying little but their dreams often go on to become superlative doctors, innovators, teachers, artists, entrepreneurs—pillars of their new communities. The free world does not "save" them; rather, it partners with them in unleashing human potential that had been previously caged. Nizam Missaghi's life is a powerful reminder of this truth.

Born into a lineage of healers, raised in a nation where his faith and identity rendered him "less than human" in the eyes of an authoritarian regime, he grew up surrounded by both extraordinary beauty and suffocating injustice. He witnessed firsthand what happens when a government decides that a certain class of people are unworthy of education, dignity, and opportunity. And yet—rather than being broken by this reality—Nizam and his family responded in a way that continues to inspire.

The Bahá'ís of Iran, whose story is woven throughout this book, represent one of the most remarkable examples of moral courage in modern history. For decades they have endured systematic persecution: loss of livelihoods, denial of education, imprisonment, even execution. And still, they have refused revenge. They have refused hatred. They have refused violence.

Instead, they have answered cruelty with loving hearts and a mindset of service.

They built underground universities when their children were barred from schools. They educated, healed, supported, and uplifted their communities quietly and constructively. They demonstrated—in real time—what it looks like to meet injustice not with bitterness, but with principled action.

In a world so addicted to outrage and retribution, this approach feels revolutionary. It is easy to speak of peace. It is much harder to live it when you are the one being oppressed. What emerges from these pages is not merely a memoir of escape. It is a testament to resilience. To the quiet heroism of parents who refused to surrender their values. To the transformative power of education. And to the profound impact that free societies can have when they open their doors to those yearning for liberty.

Nizam's journey from a child climbing stairwells during missile attacks in Tehran to becoming a top physician in the United States is not just a personal triumph—it is a story of what happens when human potential is finally allowed to breathe. It reminds us that the true wealth of nations is not oil, land, or armies. It is people. Curious minds. Compassionate hearts. Dreamers who refuse to give up even when the world tells them they don't belong. *Passport to Freedom* is ultimately about freedom—not just political freedom, but the freedom to transform into who you were destined to be. It is about how suffering, when met with courage and purpose, can give rise to extraordinary contributions to both humanity and the world. And, most of all, it is about hope—the kind of hope that doesn't wait passively for change, but actively builds it. I am honored to lend my voice to this extraordinary book.

Nizam Missaghi's story deserves to be read not only for its emotional power, but for the lessons it offers our fractured world—that compassion can outlast cruelty, that service can overcome oppression, and that when human beings are finally unchained, they don't just survive—they uplift us all. May this book inspire you.

—Rainn Wilson, February 2026

PREFACE

When I first set out to write this book, I could not have imagined its timing. A few years ago, the idea came quietly—to finally tell my story in full, to give shape to experiences that had lived inside me for decades. At the time, it felt personal, reflective, even a little overdue. I did not imagine that, as these pages came together, the United States and Iran would stand on the brink of open conflict—not a proxy war, not a shadow war, not a conflict disguised in diplomatic language or strategic ambiguity, but something more direct, more visible, more undeniable. Nor could I have anticipated that this story would arrive at a moment of symbolic convergence: as the United States marks another milestone in its national history, approaching its 250th year, and as I myself reach fifty—born in 1976, on America's bicentennial.

There is something about that symmetry that feels less like design and more like alignment. As if the personal and the historical, the individual and the collective, have found themselves moving in parallel without intention or orchestration. I am not the author of that timing, just a witness to it.

I cannot ignore the feeling that this book has, in some way, willed itself into a world that needs it now—at a moment when the distance between nations, ideologies, and lived realities feels both dangerously narrow and deeply misunderstood.

There are governments that fail their people through incompetence, and there are governments that wage war against them. The Islamic Republic of Iran has done both. From its inception, it did not merely govern badly. It declared war in many directions at once. It waged war against the Iranian people through repression, fear, humiliation, and the steady suffocation of dignity. It waged war against women by denying them sovereignty over their own bodies, denying them equal standing under the law, and even denying them the right to choose how to appear in public. Under the Islamic Republic, women did not merely become targets of social control; they became battlegrounds upon which ideology, power, and inequality were inscribed. It waged war against dissidents, students, workers, writers, environmentalists, religious minorities, ethnic minorities, and all those whose mere existence challenged the state's demand for obedience. It waged war against joy, against memory, against truth, against individuality, and against the idea that a human being might belong first to himself or herself rather than to ideology. And it did all this while speaking endlessly in the language of virtue.

For nearly half a century, the people of Iran have lived beneath a system that demanded sacrifice from everyone except those who benefited most from it. The daughters of ordinary Iranian families were stopped, fined, beaten, imprisoned, and sometimes killed over a few strands of hair, over a piece of clothing, over the simple desire to inhabit public space as free human beings. Yet the daughters and sons of those who rule in the name of austerity, piety, and anti-Western virtue often enjoyed freedoms far beyond anything permitted to the people they governed. They traveled freely. They dressed freely. They lived between worlds. They enjoyed the liberties denied to the very nation in whose name their fathers preached restriction and demanded submission.

That contradiction is not incidental. It is the essence of the system. This book was born from the long shadow of that contradiction. *Passport to Freedom* is, on one level, a personal journey: the story of leaving Iran, of uncertainty, of reinvention, of loss and becoming, of exile and belonging, of making a life in America while carrying the emotional geology of another land inside me. But it is also an account of the architecture of a system that has treated an entire nation not as citizens to be served, but as subjects to be controlled, monitored, punished, and spent.

The world often misunderstands Iran by beginning with the state. But Iran is not its rulers. Iran is not the slogans painted on missiles. Iran is not the men with rehearsed smiles, calloused foreheads, and bloodless language pretending to speak for a civilization older and nobler than they could ever comprehend. Iran is a people. A people with memory, tenderness, humor, poetry, grief, brilliance, and astonishing endurance who have had to survive not only sanctions and isolation and international misreadings, but also a relentless internal war carried out in the name of religion, revolution, and national honor. That war has taken many forms.

It has looked like prison cells, torture chambers, coerced confessions, and executions at dawn. It has looked like mothers waiting at the door for children who never returned. It has looked like the crushing of student movements, the silencing of journalists, the targeting of Baha'is, the intimidation of Christians, the narrowing of civic life, the weaponization of courts, and the dispossession of entire communities through corruption and environmental ruin. It has looked like internet blackouts imposed not simply to censor, but to blind civilians in moments of danger and deny them the ability to protect themselves. It has looked like poisoned schoolgirls, child brides, and young protesters publicly executed before they ever had a chance to become fully themselves.

It has also looked like economic violence: the collapse of currency, the destruction of predictability, the theft of opportunity, the conversion of national wealth into ideological spending, and the slow forcing of millions into exhaustion. Inflation can be a form of violence. So can corruption. The destruction of a country's future can be a form of violence. When a regime empties a nation of hope, talent, and trust, it is still waging war—even if no missile is in the sky. And yet the Islamic Republic did not confine its warfare to its own people.

From the moment of the US embassy seizure in Tehran, it established hostility not as a temporary tactic, but as an operating principle. Over the decades, it armed proxies, inflamed the region, threatened Israel openly, undermined American interests, and helped create the conditions for repeated cycles of conflict far beyond Iran's borders. It built its identity around tension, enmity, and permanent mobilization. Crisis was not a byproduct of its rule. Crisis was one of its primary instruments of legitimacy.

For years, many outside Iran treated these developments as separate stories: domestic repression over here, regional aggression over there, nuclear brinkmanship somewhere else, propaganda everywhere. But they were never separate. They were expressions of the same governing logic: a regime that survives by manufacturing fear, suppressing accountability, and externalizing the costs of its ambitions onto ordinary human beings.

Recent events have made this harder to ignore. What some describe as a sudden or unprovoked war did not emerge from a vacuum. It did not begin in a single week, or with a single strike, or with a single headline. It was the accumulated result of decades of bellicose policy, ideological obsession, proxy warfare, incitement, and strategic provocation by the Islamic Republic. This was not a war imposed on the Islamic Republic so much as yet another war imposed by the Islamic Republic—on the Iranian people first and most of all. That distinction matters because whatever one's view of military action, strategy, foreign intervention, or the actors involved, one truth remains morally unavoidable: the Iranian people did not choose these wars. They did not choose embassy seizures. They did not choose proxy militias. They did not choose slogans calling for the destruction of other nations. They did not choose economic isolation. They did not choose regional adventurism. They did not choose to have their lives tied to the obsessions of rulers who mistake ideological theater for national interest. And yet they continue to pay the price in the form of deadly missiles, hardened borders, a darkened internet, a collapsed economy. The people pay when dissent is crushed in the name of wartime unity and when the regime wraps itself in the flag after having spent decades hollowing out the nation beneath it. The Iranian people have repeatedly been made to suffer for wars they never authorized, ideologies they never consented to, and hatreds that were never theirs.

If this book has a moral center, it is this: the people of Iran are not merely caught between history and tyranny. They have been among the primary casualties of a system that has been at war—with freedom, with plurality, with accountability, and with life itself—since its earliest days. The war against the Iranian people is not an unfortunate side effect of the Islamic Republic;

it is one of its defining features. I know this not as an abstraction, but as someone shaped by that world.

I come from a country whose beauty and sorrow are inseparable in my memory. I come from a people whose greatness survived despite the machinery built to diminish them. I carry with me the tenderness of family, the discipline of survival, the ache of exile, and the enduring belief that no tyranny, however theatrical or brutal, can permanently extinguish a nation's deepest character. That belief followed me across oceans.

In America, I found opportunity, refuge, and the freedom to continue becoming. But freedom is never merely geographical. It is moral, psychological, and civilizational. It is the ability to speak without terror, to choose without coercion, to believe without compulsion, to dissent without disappearance, to love without surveillance, to dream without permission. The journey from Tehran to freedom was therefore never just a movement across borders. It was a passage from imposed identity toward chosen humanity. To tell the truth about Iran is not to dishonor it. It is to rescue it from those who have spoken in its name while betraying its people. To separate Iran from the Islamic Republic is a moral necessity.

This book exists for those who had to leave, and for those who could not. For those who survived prisons, interrogations, humiliation, and fear. For those who crossed borders with little more than talent and resolve. For those whose children now speak Persian with a foreign accent but still feel connected to their rich ancestral heritage. For those whose loved ones were executed, disappeared, silenced, or broken. For those who still dare to imagine a country where dawn does not bring terror, where law is not a disguise for vengeance, where women are not treated as lesser beings before the law, where faith is not a costume worn by opportunists, and where no government can demand that a people disappear into obedience. Above all, it exists for the Iranian people—the ultimate victims of the Islamic Republic, but never merely its victims.

It also exists for the American people: for those who may never have had to flee a homeland, never had to measure their words in fear, never had to ask permission to think, dress, worship, speak, or dream freely. It exists as an invitation to understand more deeply the foundations of liberty they have inherited, and the sacrifices made by generations before them that helped build a land of extraordinary opportunity.

At the close of the Constitutional Convention in 1787, when asked what kind of government had been created, Benjamin Franklin replied: "A republic, if you can keep it." It was not a casual remark. It was a warning—and a responsibility. It is a reminder that freedom is not self-sustaining, but requires vigilance and demands participation. Freedom can erode slowly, quietly, almost invisibly—until one day, it is no longer recognizable. This book exists, in part, to illuminate what that erosion looks like when it is left unchecked. A cautionary tale to show how rights can be narrowed, truth distorted, institutions hollowed out, and how a people can gradually be separated from their own voice. *Passport to Freedom* exists as a quiet but urgent appeal to safeguard what has been built—not only for the present, but for future generations who will inherit either the strength or the fragility of that republic.

It exists, too, as a tribute to the welcoming culture of America—a culture that has allowed immigrants, generation after generation, not only to find refuge and possibility, but also to give back, build, heal, create, and strengthen the country that received them. America enriches the life of the immigrant, and immigrants, in turn, enrich America. That mutuality is one of the great achievements of a free society.

PART I

LOOKING BACK

CHAPTER 1

When I was ten years old, my world fit into the stairwell of our four-story walk-up in Tehran, the time-worn capital of Iran. It was 1986, and for weeks, the newspapers hitting the glass-paned front door each morning boasted headlines of the coming of Halley's Comet. Now the universe would be viewable from my own window! Waiting for my father to roll the rubber band off the folded newspaper, I'd anticipate the headlines that had started weeks before the big event: "Visions of Halley's Comet," "Here Comes Halley," and then one that captured my imagination most: "Eyes on the Sky, How to Watch Halley's Comet without a Telescope."

The delivery boy pedaled up our narrow street every morning, balancing a "Breaking News" bundle on the handlebars. Sometimes the paper hit the balcony glass with a loud thwack. I would grab it, inhaling the sharp, slightly metallic scent of fresh ink and paper, and place it carefully on the table for my father.

Halley was not just a comet; she was a time traveler. Scientists said she came every seventy-five or seventy-six years, trailing her ice and dust across human generations. The last time she had appeared, Mark Twain had been alive to write about her. The time before that, Charles Darwin was researching his theory of evolution. Halley carried not only a future with her but a history, too, and I wanted to be a part of both.

Before 1986, the last time Halley's Comet had visited the Iranian sky was in 1910, when history books say the comet was visible to the naked eye. It was not only the heavens that shimmered with new light but the nation itself. A fresh middle class—teachers, merchants, journalists, and reformers—was taking shape, daring to imagine a modern Iran grounded in education, equality, and participation. A revolution was underway then, known as the Constitutional Revolution. Little did the revolutionaries of 1910 know that their movement would remain unfinished, derailed by the clerical establishment. But for a moment, the country had its own visibility—both outward to the world and inward to its own potential. Like the comet streaking bright and brief across the darkness, that visibility illuminated a path toward progress, showing Iranians what could be. When Halley's Comet returned in 1986, I could not help but wonder whether the light might signal a new awakening once more. Could Iran again emerge from the shadows—this time not just to be seen, but to see itself clearly?

Halley carried history, a streak of light that had witnessed generations long before mine, and now she returned to witness me. I imagined that same comet blazing across the skies above distant lands, connecting me—a boy in Tehran—to children my age in Paris, Tokyo, or New York. It was a thread linking past and future. She had seen it all, and she'd see more, beyond one child's lifetime. If I didn't see the comet now, I might never see it. Even as a child, I was aware I could be dead by the next pass, if not much sooner, from Iraqi missiles raining on Tehran. And yet, I imagined our conversation as a man in my mid-eighties:

when she returned, I would tell how the world had changed—that children did not have to live through war, that they would not be dismissed from school, that mothers could work freely and choose how to dress, that families could be safe, that life would be fair. I was making a pact with a cosmic time capsule. When I saw her again one day, I'd remember who I was when I first laid eyes on her, and I'd give thanks for how far we had both come.

I marked my Page-a-Day calendar, wrote down the pre-dawn hours, and set my twin-bell alarm clock. At three or four in the morning, I would climb the four flights of stairs, feeling the cool concrete beneath my bare feet. Upward, the staircase led to the roof, where I could reach for the heavens. Downward, the same set of stairs offered protection when the raid sirens screamed, shielding us from the threat of falling glass from Iraqi bombs as the Iran-Iraq war escalated. That staircase held both danger and promise. It also led to our small, shared backyard, where a magnolia tree stood in the center. Over the years, it grew so tall that even from the second floor, we could smell the fragrance of its large white flowers during bloom season. When we were young, just learning to ride bicycles without training wheels, we would circle the magnolia tree for hours on end, laughing as we went round and round. Sometimes, if a bud had opened, we would cut it, place it in a glass of water on the kitchen table, and watch it bloom inside the house, filling our home with its scent.

At the table, my father smoothed out the creases of his newspaper. Dad was a man of rituals. He would sit there in the mornings and on weekends, enormous black-and-white pages spread before him, his glasses perched on the edge of his long nose, his hands gripping the paper so the only part of him you could see was his feet peeking from underneath the table.

When I was younger, I thought my father was a news junkie. But looking back, I realize he wasn't addicted to news; he was addicted to the truth. Every evening, he'd tune in to the official broadcasts everyone in Iran was expected to watch. They were monotonous and predictable—full of slogans, praise for the Ayatollah, and carefully edited stories that were designed to keep people obedient. But he listened anyway. He wanted to know exactly what they were saying and how the regime wanted us to think.

Later at night, though, his real listening began. He'd take out his transistor radio, a small silver one he'd brought back from Austria years earlier after visiting his older brother, who had immigrated there and lived freely. That radio meant a lot to my father. It was a gift from his brother and, in a way, a connection to the free world he longed for.

The government tried to block outside news with heavy interference, which we called *parazit*, meaning "parasite" to describe the static we heard. When my father turned the dial, the air filled with that crackling noise, like metal grinding against itself. Still, he'd lean in close, pressing the radio to his ear, adjusting the dial until a voice began to break through the static: "This is the Voice of America in Persian," or sometimes, "This is BBC Persian." Those faint words felt almost forbidden.

For my father, listening to those broadcasts wasn't just about staying informed; it was about staying connected to truth itself. His Bahá'í faith teaches that truthfulness is the foundation of all virtues, and lying for self-preservation is forbidden, even when the cost is high. Most Bahá'ís refuse to hide their faith on job or school applications, even though it might mean losing opportunities. My parents were no different. They believed that if a society ever hoped to move forward, it had to start with honesty.

That belief stood in stark contrast to the culture around us. Within the Shi'a establishment, deceit had been redefined as a strategy. There were religious justifications for it—*taqiyya*, the idea of concealing the truth to protect yourself, and *khod'eh*, strategic deception. Over time, these became normalized ways of operating. Even language was twisted to make wrong things sound right. It was a system built on the manipulation of words and, eventually, on the erosion of truth itself.

So when my father sat at the table late at night, holding that little Austrian radio close to his ear, it wasn't just a hobby. It was a quiet act of resistance. Through all that static, he was listening for clarity.

I always carried in my heart a hope for change. I believed that one day, the regime of the Islamic Republic would be uninstalled as easily as it seemed to have been installed, and freedom and equality would become our new normal. That was a version of the future that even Halley could not promise, but it was a hope I held onto. I thought I just needed to be patient and wait until it all changed. Hopefully, it would be by the time I graduated high school, so I wouldn't be denied access to higher education because of my faith.

I knew very young that I wanted to be a doctor like my mother and her ancestors. I saw the way she calmed sick children, how her patients left with hope stitched into their voices, and how she handed each of them candy at the end of each visit. But I also knew, too young, that unless things changed, becoming a doctor was impossible for me in Iran. Having been born to a Bahá'í family, I was among the "unclean." Bahá'ís were (and still are) among the religious minorities in Iran and could not, because of the strict discriminatory policy of the Islamic Republic, enroll in any university, much less medical school. They could not become scientists, lawyers, or professors. Dreams were barred at the door of the university.

So, I just kept believing that, certainly by the time I was eighteen, the majority of people living in the country would have had enough—that there'd be an uprising, the people would win, and everyone would have access to learning. The end.

Maybe I thought the oppression would leave with Halley and she'd return to me with a happy ending. I could ask her to carry the nonsensical rules and regulations away from my home and into a faraway universe, so I could claim a world of my own. If I could be patient enough to reach a time and place where Bahá'ís could study and become doctors, I would know she had delivered my dream back to me. Halley traveled, so one day I would too.

* * *

In post-revolutionary Iran, anyone who didn't conform to the rules of the Islamic Republic was branded an infidel and stripped of their rights. As you will read, my family comes from a long line of people who find it impossible to stray from their values or to be disingenuous, even if doing so would make their lives more comfortable. Every basic human freedom—education, work, pension, even the right to own a business—hung in the balance for those who dared to dissent. People like us lived under constant scrutiny. Passports were denied, travel was restricted, and escape—both literal and spiritual—was almost impossible. We were called "non-humans," members of an unrecognized "religious minority," as if faith itself had demoted us from full personhood.

The story of the Bahá'í faith begins in nineteenth-century Persia. They were a society caught between ancient tradition and the first tremors of modernity. It was a time of spiritual restlessness when people longed for renewal and justice in an era of rigid hierarchy and division. Out of that longing emerged Bahá'u'lláh, the founder of the Bahá'í faith, whose message was both revolutionary and timeless: humanity is one, the world's religions come from the same divine source, and universal peace depends on recognizing this oneness.

Bahá'u'lláh's teachings were radical for their time. He called for equality between men and women, for the harmony of science and religion, and for universal education as a birthright—not privileges reserved for the elite. These were not abstract ideals but practical blueprints for a just society. Yet progress often provokes fear. Persia's clerical establishment and government viewed the Bahá'ís as heretics and political threats. The early believers faced persecution, imprisonment, and executions, but they refused violence, choosing steadfast faith over retaliation. Their quiet endurance became a new kind of resistance—rooted in dignity, unity, and love.

To be a Bahá'í in that time meant to live under suspicion and to be excluded from opportunity while keeping one's heart open. My ancestors were among those who held fast to these principles. Their stories—of courage, sacrifice, and grace under pressure—became the invisible scaffolding of my own moral world. When I think of the early Bahá'ís, I think of what it means to remain gentle in a brutal time and to stand upright in a storm of intolerance.

It was this same spirit of sacrifice that I recognized in my own family history. My paternal great-grandfather, Nizam, whom I am named after, embodied the same steadfast devotion a century earlier. He willingly became a Bahá'í after being raised Muslim. A skilled calligrapher, he used his talents to publish Bahá'í writings during the Qajar era despite the laws that criminalized such acts. His courage landed him in jail, and he faced the very real possibility of execution for standing by his beliefs. But following the shelling of the parliament in 1908 by Mohammad Ali Shah, political prisoners, including Nizam, were released, and he continued his work in the service of his faith and in the oneness of people.

The Bahá'í vision of humanity's oneness was more than a creed; it was a way of seeing. It shaped how my family treated others across boundaries of faith and culture, and how I would later come to understand myself—half Iranian, part Jewish, raised among Muslims and Bahá'ís, born in New York. Long before I could name it, that idea of oneness was already written into my story.

My mother was born Tahereh Berjis. And being a Berjis, my mother was destined to be a doctor. Nobody would take that away from her. My mother hailed from generations of physicians and healers as far back as the family tree has been recorded. Berjis translates to "Jupiter," the largest planet with a gravitational power that attracts ninety-five moons to her orbit. My mother was our gravitational influence, in our home and in our community. We circled around her brilliance, her compassion, and her natural ability as a healer. Patients flocked to her, as did students of science and literature. My mother's sacrifice to care for her community at any cost upheld her family's dedication to the profession and planted the seed in me that I would one day follow in their footsteps.

Jupiter is also known for its persistent storm, which can be seen through a telescope, known as the Great Red Spot. There were many times I would see this persistent storm inside my mother's heart unleash in the form of silent protest against anyone or anything that threatened her dignity. Her heart was her own big red spot.

The Berjis family of doctors shared blood with literal martyrs who sacrificed to remain true to their values. I used to dream about meeting my great uncle, Dr. Sulayman Berjis, who had been brutally murdered by Islamic zealots in 1950, long before the Iranian Revolution. His death left an indelible mark on our family. I imagined my mother kept her uncle in mind as she set up her exam table, adamant, to honor his legacy. Iran itself was (and is) beautiful. I don't want to tell you only about oppression and fear. Despite war, prejudice, bigotry, and Sharia law, the streets of Tehran still pulsed with life. The bazaars overflowed with saffron and pistachios, and pomegranates cracked open into gardens of rubies. In the spring, tulips bloomed behind high walls, roses and jasmine filling the air at dusk. The scent of freshly baked bread mingled with the smoky aroma of street grills, fruits, and vegetables on stands with colors so bright, they looked like an edible crayon box. Children ran between the legs of women with flowing scarves, their laughter ringing above the rhythm of bicycle bells. The Alborz mountains watched over us, snow-capped and eternal.

And then the call to prayer, the sound of the *muezzin* emerging from the minaret of nearby mosques, could be heard in every corner. The architecture of the city was a patchwork of eras: elegant brickwork from the Qajar dynasty, whitewashed modernist apartments rising beside ancient courtyards, domes and minarets punctuating the horizon. Colorful tiles shimmered in the sun on mosque walls and market façades, mosaics like tiny pieces of a starry sky. On Fridays, the sounds of prayers echoed faintly from distant mosques, a reminder that all lived within this Islamic Republic regardless of background or creed.

Posters of the watchful eye of Ayatollah Khomeini, the Supreme Leader, lined the sides of buildings, brick walls, and billboards. Soldiers occasionally patrolled, a reminder that freedom could be curtailed in an instant and that there was only one accepted cultural and religious way of life in Iran. Dissidents were the enemy, even a ten-year-old like me. Nobody, not even some of my teachers, let me forget it.

Smoke from distant bombings sometimes mingled with the city's usual smells, a harsh scent layered over the spices and frying breads. And yet, through it all, life continued. Children played hopscotch and marbles in the alleys, women carried groceries home, and restaurants buzzed with whispered conversations.

It was a city of paradoxes, both alive and constrained. From my perch on the roof, I could watch it all: the way light glinted off the copper domes despite the haze of smoke and smog. And I imagined that somewhere far above, Halley's Comet was about to streak across the sky, carrying the possibility that someday, things could be different.

It was 1986. Iraq had been at war with Iran for six years. The warning sirens became ubiquitous to the daily rhythm of life. Sometimes we would crouch in the stairwell, pressing our backs to the concrete walls, as the muffled thuds of missiles struck somewhere nearby. The stairwell was windowless and reinforced—both a sanctuary and a path. I would climb it toward the hope of Halley's Comet and retreat down it toward survival.

Even at night, the sky was cloudy. Some nights, the light pollution from the streets, the haze of the city, or the gray of smog hid everything. I had no visibility to the stars or Halley.

The disappointment stung but didn't stunt my hope. I'd keep climbing the stairs. This was the paradox of my childhood—a country radiant with unmatched beauty, history, and culture, yet one that narrowed my own future because I was not of the right belief.

* * *

Our apartment itself was a mix of acceptance and rebellion, literature and music. My room was a small shrine to what the outside world could be if the Islamic Republic were not in charge of the country and our laws. Posters of Madonna and Boy George plastered the walls of my room, vibrant and defiant against the void of popular music outside. In the corner of our living room, a German-made Gründig VCR stood, as heavy as a small child, its rectangular tapes thick and precious. We had only seven or eight video relics of pre-revolution Iran: music videos of singers, men and women without headscarves, performing at parties, laughing together. I had memorized every song and every dance, rewound and played them again and again, a secret window into a freer world that existed prior to 1979.

Our upstairs neighbor, Mr. Zohrehnejad, had a Betamax—the precursor to VHS—and he rigged a coaxial splitter to share his VCR output within the building. At night, families gathered around televisions, waiting for the auxiliary channel to flicker to life. Sometimes he would be a few minutes late, and we would fidget in anticipation, the tension pulsating through all four floors. When the screen came alive, it was another universe: *Top Gun, Picket Fences,* American and Australian series and movies, music videos…colorful explosions of sound and image. Watching Macaulay Culkin's character in *Home Alone*—where a young boy is left to face the world of adults and intruders on his own—stirred something deep in me. I identified with him instinctively. The outside world felt like a realm ruled entirely by grown-ups who only understood power in their own terms and saw a young boy like me as a misfit—a young Bahá'í child who was different from the narrative they wished to fashion for a future homogenous generation. They held all the authority, all the force. And like Kevin in that empty house, we learned to survive not by confronting power head-on, but through craft, quiet resilience, and clever detours and workarounds. We found ways to move forward, to get our education, to remain unseen when necessary, and yet, in our own small ways, to resist and push back whenever we could.

I remember watching MTV and the video for Culture Club's "Karma Chameleon," the colors in the video so vivid—the stripes on Boy George's jacket, the braids in his hair, the blues of the sky in a place called Mississippi, his lipstick and eye liner, the sound of the harmonica…it felt unreal, like a dream I could touch. And MC Hammer had a song about precisely that.

I also remember the first time I saw MC Hammer on MTV, with his baggy pants, slick dance moves, and a beat that made you want to bounce, even if you didn't understand the words. He kept repeating, "Can't touch this," and I understood enough English to repeat it too. But I couldn't figure out what it meant. *What can't we touch?* I kept looking at the screen, trying to spot in vain the thing everyone was apparently forbidden to touch.

It would take me years to understand that he wasn't talking about an object at all. He meant *himself*—his talent, his rhythm, his swagger. No one could touch *that.* But back then, I just saw this joyful chaos of people in parachute pants doing the same dance against a white background, and I thought, *Whatever it is we can't touch, everyone seems happy about it.*

We eventually pooled our money with neighbors to buy a satellite dish. We turned it toward the sky, greedy for forbidden signals. Through that dish, my mother devoured *The Thorn Birds,* practicing her English and connecting to a Western culture she had briefly been a part of as a medical resident in New York. She also watched ice skating with a passion. She called it *patinage,* the French word. Whenever a skating competition came on, she was mesmerized. I remember being thirteen, sitting cross-legged next to her, watching women in glittery, revealing costumes spin across the ice. Their bodysuits clung to them, their hair in tight buns, their faces uncovered. I whispered, half-shocked, half-admiring, "These women are absolutely beautiful. Are you looking at the men?" My mother laughed, eyes never leaving the screen. "Are you kidding? I'm also looking at the women."

Outside, we lived under a regime that reduced women to shadows. Inside, we witnessed a world where women could soar, spin, dazzle. The difference weighed on me.

The other thing my mom loved was the Oscars. Every once in a while, a tape of the ceremony would show up or the award ceremony would air through satellite, and she'd watch it, even if she hadn't seen most of the nominated movies. For her, it wasn't about the films; it was about the clothes, the style, the presentation. She loved watching the celebrities on the red carpet, how the presenters carried themselves to the podium in cadence to the orchestra and how elegant the whole event was. She'd sometimes take the taped ceremony to her tailor and point to a dress or a neckline she liked. "Can you make me something like this?" she'd say. She rarely shopped in stores because she hated the idea of showing up to a gathering and finding someone else wearing the same outfit. She had her own taste—very distinct, very proud. I can still see her showing the seamstress Meryl Streep's gown and saying, "Something like this, but in my color."

I'll never forget seeing the video for *Thriller* for the first time through that coaxial cable running from our upstairs neighbor's VCR. It was pure magic. The transformation scene, when Michael turns from a teenager to a werewolf, blew our minds, especially the ending, when Michael turns to the camera with glowing eyes and laughs that eerie, devilish laugh. It left an itch in my brain.

But what really stuck with me was that moment in the video for Billie Jean, when Michael danced on the sidewalk, and each tile lit up as he stepped. For weeks after, on my way to school, I'd try to walk the same way, hopping from one tile to the next, pretending they were lighting up under my feet. To anyone watching, I must've looked ridiculous. But to me, it felt like I was walking in the same world he was.

The regime called these things a cultural invasion. But to me, the music, the fashion, the entertainment, and the sport all felt like freedom with a touch of magic breaking through. And if that was an invasion, I remember thinking, *I wouldn't mind being invaded more often*. If anything, I felt that the imposition of the Islamic Republic's values and codes on every facet of my life was the biggest "cultural invasion."

Some of the television I watched with a twinge of envy. Other times, it was pure imagination. I'd picture myself there, in that place, living that life. Even celebrities, who always seemed larger than life, became relatable in small ways. Watching *Phil Donahue* or *Oprah* with their aspirational theme songs, I'd focus on the audience. They were ordinary people, just like me. And I'd think, *If I were in America, I could be sitting there too.*

Adults in Iran had real problems: war, survival, exorbitant and dynamic inflation, political, religious, and sexual oppression, home raids, and difficulty finding work. But at ten years old, I had a simpler, desperate hope: to witness Halley's Comet with my own eyes, to chart and track her, to make a pact with her that one day Iran would wiggle its way out from under the thumb of the Islamic Republic. If I could have pulled Halley from the sky and bottled her promise forever, I would have.

The Iran-Iraq War intruded. Tehran nights were split by the low moan of sirens and the fear that Iraqi missiles would find their mark. Sometimes the power went out, and we sat in candlelight while my father fiddled with the dials of his battery powered short-wave radio, searching for BBC Persian, Voice of America, Radio Israel—any station that slipped through the government's jamming. That crackling voice in the dark felt like another comet, a signal from far away proclaiming that life could be different.

The Iran–Iraq War was fought not only on the frontlines—it seeped into our living rooms, our classrooms, our kitchens, and the very rhythm of our childhood. Among its most suffocating legacies were the rolling blackouts, those nightly plunges into darkness that swallowed entire neighborhoods without warning.

For a schoolchild trying to study, it felt like the war had followed us home. Evenings were the hardest. You never knew how much time you had before the lights flickered once, twice, and surrendered. Families lit candles, the little flames trembling against the cold drafts that swept through the house. Wealthier neighbors sometimes had generators, a luxury whose loud hum felt like another reminder of how unequal life could be. But even those machines could rarely power more than a few bulbs—certainly not a freezer, which meant food spoiled often, long before anyone could use it.

Winter made everything worse. Most homes relied on electrical thermostats to activate the heater, and without electricity, the system simply died. Our house grew so cold some nights that your breath showed in the air. My father—resourceful as always—brought home a gas-powered heater and set it up in the living room. Then he did something ingenious: He ran a copper pipe off the heater and installed a small gas-powered lamp. That single lamp became our sun.

Every evening, we gathered around that heater the way ancient families once gathered around a fire. The warmth was uneven, the light was dim, but it was enough to study by. Enough to keep our fingers from stiffening as we held our pencils. Enough to convince ourselves that life still had structure and progress was still possible.

Even the simplest needs became delicate negotiations with the electric grid. A warm shower required waiting—sometimes hours—until the power surged back and the water heater came to life. We learned to listen for the click of appliances coming back to life, a sound that felt like hope announcing its brief return.

These blackouts framed our childhood in the 1980s. They taught us discipline and patience, but also a kind of improvisational survival. We grew up doing homework by candlelight, warming our hands over a sputtering gas flame, racing to shower before the next outage, and learning—far too young—that even ordinary life could be a battlefield when a country was at war.

The great irony of my life was that I had actually been born free—an American citizen—in the same New York hospital where my mother was completing her pediatric residency. When my mother's training ended, we returned to Iran. For the first three months of my life, I belonged to a world where freedom was assumed and where the matter of my parents' faith was no matter at all. It took me years to realize that the freedom I'd been born into and the faith I was born from were bound by the same truth: Both began as radical ideas in places that didn't yet know how to hold them. And like Halley's Comet, glimpses of hope can appear briefly, passing overhead and vanishing into darkness. But they leave a trail—a reminder of where you came from and what you might one day find again.

CHAPTER 2

My story began not in the mountains of Iran but in the bustling streets of New York City, where my mother was finishing her residency, and my father was learning how to be both a parent and a partner. They had left Iran for educational opportunity, never knowing the choices they made then would chart the course of my escape years later.

"Let's have another baby," my father said to my mother, handing her a brown-bagged lunch. My one-and-a-half-year-old sister sat on the burnt-orange carpeting—a sign of the seventies—opening and closing her fist in a clumsy wave goodbye. My mother, eyes puffy from too little sleep, was heading out for another long shift at New York Infirmary Hospital where she was a pediatric resident. She leaned on my father not just for support, but for everything: childcare, cooking, keeping their small household afloat.

They were sacrificing for each other in different ways. My mother was laser-focused on finishing her residency, determined to become a licensed pediatrician despite the toll it took on her body and her time with her first child. My father, an engineer, had set aside his own career to become a full-time parent so she could pursue her dream.

Both were already highly educated scholars when they left Iran for America, hoping New York would be a stepping stone rather than a permanent home. The plan had always been to return to Iran when my mother's residency ended in June 1976. But they also wanted two children—both born in the United States.

"I want our children to have options," my father said, coaxing her toward the idea. "They will be Persian, citizens of Iran, but with US citizenship, they'll have choices when they're older."

This kind of partnership was natural to them, rooted in their Bahá'í faith. My father saw no shame in swapping traditional roles, and my mother relied on him fully. Their marriage reflected their faith: progressive, but invisible to the Iranian state. Even before the Islamic Revolution, Bahá'í marriages were not officially recognized, making everything from buying a home to proving their union a bureaucratic struggle. My mother, never silent when it came to dignity, would collect affidavits from neighbors or write letters to prove what the state refused to acknowledge. In America, though, their word and their paperwork were enough. Ironically, they could have lived together unmarried in New York without question, but that was a kind of freedom my parents had no appetite for.

By the spring of 1975, the clock was ticking in more than one way. My mother's J1 visa and residency would expire by the end of the following June. If she were to conceive, it would have to be then, or her second child would be born in Iran without the "options" my father had meticulously devised.

New York in spring is fragrant with renewal, and in late March of 1976, I arrived with the equinox, born at the very hospital where my mother trained. My birth coincided with Nowruz, the Persian New Year, a holiday symbolizing new beginnings. In Iran, Nowruz would have been marked by family gatherings, gift exchanges, and shared meals. In New York, it was quieter, lonelier. "In a country where nobody recognized Nowruz," my parents told me, "you were our holiday gift."

But their true "new day" was waiting back home in their country. With my mother's pediatric training complete and my father ready to return to engineering, they looked forward to immersing my sister and me in Iran's rich culture and contributing to their homeland with the tools America had given them.

On July 4, 1976, as the United States wrapped itself in red, white, and blue for the bicentennial of its Revolution, my parents packed our bags. The very next day, they presented me—three months old, with an American passport in hand—to Iranian border agents. I was, in the most literal sense, an American in Tehran.

Even then, pre-revolutionary Iran was a country of contrasts. For my parents and their peers, it was a place of opportunity, a land where education and science flourished. Universities such as Aryamehr University of Technology and the University of Tehran were producing engineers, doctors, and scientists who sought to propel Iran into modernity. Many students traveled abroad to the United States and Europe, returning with degrees, visions, and ambitions to rebuild their homeland.

Among them were individuals who would later become heroes in my eyes. Mahmoud Badavam, an MIT-trained engineer, had returned to Iran to contribute despite having the option to remain abroad. After the Revolution, he was dismissed from his position because of his Bahá'í faith, yet he still found a way to teach in the Bahá'í Institute for Higher Education, helping students barred from university. For his dedication, he served five years in prison. And still, he persevered, demonstrating how commitment to one's community could survive even under the harshest circumstances. When he came to our house to teach with my mother, my sister and I would ask him to tell stories of his time in the US—about his life in Boston and his experiences at MIT. We wanted a taste of America, right there in Tehran, from someone who had sacrificed so much to be with us.

Shamil Zargham, a renowned architect who designed the Iranian embassy in Beijing—the largest Iranian embassy in the world at the time—was another example. His license revoked after the Revolution because he was a Bahá'í, he turned to watercolor painting to survive. Every time I saw his work hung on a wall in our home, I thought about the nation's loss: a man whose skill and imagination could have shaped skylines now constrained to selling paintings. It was clear to me even as a child: The true treasure of a nation is its people—their minds and imaginations, not its oil or natural resources. This was the story of brain drain in Iran.

Amid these stories of brilliance and deprivation, I was also shaped by the quiet strength of my maternal grandmother, Monireh Khanum. In Persian, Monireh means illumined. We called her Monir for short. Khanum simply means "lady" and is used as a way to show respect for a woman—it can be added to anyone's name as a term of respect. So, her name was essentially Illumined Lady, and Monir lived up to this name. Monir had grown up Jewish but married my grandfather, becoming Bahá'í out of respect and faith, while retaining her Jewish identity in culture and thought. She was educated and had served as a school principal during her adult life, a rarity for a woman of her time. She had her own language for understanding the world: to distinguish Muslim friends from the Jewish and Bahá'í community, she would use the Hebrew word "goyim." Persian speakers would not catch on, but members of the family knew what she meant. She had other sayings, too, one of which stayed with me. When I greeted her, "Hello, Grandmother, how are you?" she would reply, "More of it is gone, less of it is left."

I thought she meant the day. I didn't know she meant her life.

Monir Khanum was very graceful. She'd had cataract surgery, and back then, there were no intraocular lenses. So, she had these big, thick-bottomed, Coke-bottle glasses. She looked so old with veins bulging from beneath the skin on her bruised hands, which is why her deepest blessing also sounded like a curse: "May you grow old." At the time, we thought she was mocking us with the idea of frailty and decay. Later, I realized her wish was one for our survival; growing old meant living a full life despite the forces of war, persecution, and uncertainty that surrounded us.

When she passed, her brother Elias, who had changed his name to Iraj to avoid persecution as a Jew, hosted her memorial in his Jewish home. Though he had remained Jewish, he asked my mother to conduct the service with Bahá'í readings. Jews, Bahá'ís, and Muslims came together, united in grief and respect. For a moment, there were no divisions, no labels—just shared humanity—a humanity I had hardly witnessed in the outside world. But when I did, it felt like being handed a passport of a different type—one that would later be stamped by the faces and hands of those who would help me find my way to freedom, education, and prosperity.

* * *

My mother marched through the living room carrying a six-foot-tall wooden partition, leaned it against the wall, and marched back out the front door. A minute later, she returned with another partition, my father trailing behind with boxes of medical and office supplies, or so the story goes. I was a toddler when my parents built a makeshift medical office in our modest apartment. Less than three years after our return to Iran, after the 1979 Revolution, the Ayatollah Khomeini was installed. The US Embassy in Tehran was raided and boarded up, and my parents, along with other "religious minorities" and dissidents opposed to Sharia law, were fired from their professions. The big red storm in my mother's heart ignited.

Ultimately, it didn't matter how skilled or compassionate my mother had been in treating children. Nor did her US training, devotion, positive outcomes, or hospital-wide modernization of care. She was dismissed from her prestigious position at a hospital in Tehran simply because she was Bahá'í. That firing marked more than the loss of a job; it marked the beginning of a systematic erasure of the Bahá'í community from public life. Under the newly established Islamic Republic, we were branded heretics—"non-humans"—and treated as though our faith stripped us of personhood itself. There had been prejudice and bigotry before, but now, the word "Bahá'í" began to sound like a curse.

And yet, my mother did not collapse under the weight of injustice. With her Big Red Spot, she upheld the central principle of the Bahá'í faith—non-violence, even in the face of oppression. Her form of civil disobedience was persistence and mastering the art of the workaround: building a door within the walls that were closing in. My mother did this quietly. One could never quite know what was going on in her active mind. Often, she'd appear present during meals or family gatherings, but then her hazel eyes would drift into a faraway gaze, signaling she was working something out—solving problems in another dimension where possibility still existed.

Together, my parents created a sanctuary in our home. Outside our apartment door hung a plaque that read: *Dr. T. Berjis, Specialist in Pediatrics from the USA.* It was her differentiator in an otherwise generic alleyway, meant to reassure patients, but to me, it was a reminder of what had been stolen from her. She set up her makeshift office off the formal living room where her exam table and her desk were placed along with a small fridge with an infant scale for babies. Her stethoscope was draped over a leather office chair, and the formal dining room had become the waiting area where her secretary would check the patients in. Families brought their children with full confidence during her office hours in the afternoon, knowing she was skilled and knowing that she was vulnerable.

What I didn't yet understand was that what happened to my mother was not an isolated injustice. It was the ripple of a nation coming undone.

In 1979, Iran's Revolution swept through the country like wildfire. On the surface, it was the people's victory—a revolt against the Shah's absolute power and excess. But like all revolutions, it was more complicated than the slogans painted on city walls. Beneath the chants and flags, powerful invisible currents electrified. Foreign powers tugged at the strings; the Cold War loomed. The Shah, once a Western ally, had grown too independent, too strong at the helm of OPEC, too ambitious in controlling oil prices and charting Iran's future. And in the vacuum of trust and leadership, a cleric in exile—Ayatollah

Khomeini—rose to power, his return orchestrated as much by world politics as by religious supremacy.

People stormed the US Embassy. The streets of Tehran developed a new voice—not the familiar hum of buses and vendors and schoolchildren, but a raw, restless chant filled with Anti-American slogans that seemed to rise and fall like an unpredictable tide. To my four-year-old ears, it didn't sound political. It sounded like chaos trying to speak in human language.

Men filled the sidewalks, some with clenched fists raised, others with expressions I didn't yet have names for—anger, excitement, fear, or something that hovered uncomfortably between them. Everything felt tense. Sometimes, walking to the market, the adults would pull me closer, tightening their grip on my hand as if I might accidentally dissolve into the crowd.

On the television, the same images returned again and again. Young men climbing over the tall iron gates of the American embassy. Faces covered. Windows shattered. Papers scattered like snow across the ground. But according to the voice of the state broadcaster, it wasn't chaos. It was victory. The revolutionaries triumphantly called the embassy "the den of spies."

Even at that age, I noticed the strange mismatch between the voice and the images. The announcer's tone was triumphant, almost celebratory, as if narrating a national football win. But on the screen, faces were hard, frantic, and charged with something darker. I didn't know the word for propaganda yet, but I could feel its discomfort. The images of blindfolded American embassy workers, diplomats, and civilians, were repeatedly shown on television as some prized accomplishment of the fledgling Islamic Republic. Those sixty-six people became Iran's hostages.

When the Shah fell and the Ayatollah, or Supreme Leader, took his place, Iran was promised moral renewal and justice for the poor with characteristic populist speeches. But what arrived instead was a new kind of tyranny—one cloaked in religion that reached into homes, classrooms, and even brainwashed hearts. The ideals of freedom and equality were replaced with rules of purity and obedience, couched as the law of Allah—Sharia Law. Overnight, a nation that had glimpsed modernity turned its gaze back to stone.

For families like ours, the shift was tectonic. My parents, both educated and modern, suddenly found themselves on the wrong side of faith. The Bahá'í community became a target for persecution. Teachers, doctors, engineers…all stripped of their professions, their pensions, their dignity, and even their lives. In the name of God, the regime erased everything it deemed impure.

When the Revolution came, it didn't just change our government; it changed the air we breathed. Iran's Bahá'í community—already viewed with suspicion under the Shah—became the new regime's favorite scapegoat. The Islamic Republic declared us heretics. Overnight, neighbors looked away. Employers stopped calling. Teachers whispered.

The new laws stripped Bahá'ís of their rights to work, study, or even to be buried with dignity. Students were expelled from universities and professionals erased from their careers. Home loans were halted, bank accounts frozen, businesses shuttered or forced to place signs on their storefronts: "Operated By a Religious Minority," a scarlet letter for all to see. An Armenian-owned Christian pastry shop owner had to display a conspicuous "religious minority" sign since they handled food, lest a "pious Muslim" sin by purchasing pastries there. The shop owners seemed to view their mandatory sign as advertising their business's cleanliness and quality since everyone in the neighborhood knew them to uphold the highest professional standard while being exposed to the most scrutiny by the health department. My mother's office did not have to display a sign. Within the neighborhood, it was well known that she was a religious minority, but her reputation and the quality of care she provided seemed to matter more than her religion.

The sign wasn't just about persecution; it was erasure.

Soon after my mother was fired, my father, an English scholar with a master's degree in plant genetics and agronomy, lost his employment with a French pipe and gas company based in Tehran after it abruptly shut down its operations. He eventually found work at a paint manufacturing company, far removed from what he had been used to. "My specialty is working outside of my specialty," he would joke.

The Bahá'ís did not answer with rage or rebellion. That was never their way. Instead, they turned inward and upward toward service, learning, and unity. When universities slammed their doors, the community built a new one from scratch. From living rooms and basements across Iran, they founded what became known as the Bahá'í Institute for Higher Education—an unofficial university, elusive to the regime but very real to those who taught and studied there.

My parents were among its founders. My father helped design and teach the curriculum; my mother taught classes and mentored young women and men who had been denied a future. My mother's medical bag sat beside stacks of exam papers. The same room where she prescribed remedies for the sick now held anatomy and embryology charts and lesson plans. They were not educators by profession, but they were believers in action.

In those days, our kitchen became a place of quiet defiance—a Headquarters of the Workaround. The regime believed that stripping people of their rights would weaken them, but it had the opposite effect. Deprivation bred ingenuity. Isolation became alliance. What was meant to silence us instead galvanized an underground network of families determined to help one another and to make sure the next generation not only survived, but thrived.

In our family, you did not fight oppression by shouting. You built something the oppressor could not destroy. That belief—that action mattered more than anger—was stitched into the fabric of my childhood. I didn't know it then, but my parents and community had taught me that faith without action was hollow. When the time came, I would learn what that meant.

The Revolution had overturned everything. In its wake, survival became a language we all had to learn, passed quietly from one generation to the next. And just as we began to grasp the rules of this new world, war came only a year later—loud, relentless, uninvited—pressing its weight on our city, our streets, our homes. Life piled disaster upon disaster, testing courage, patience, and hope, especially for a child. Yet, amid the chaos, we discovered something vital: the human instinct to adapt, to create order where none was offered, and to build invisible networks of care and protection. The lessons of the hidden, quiet, and clever became our inheritance, a family blueprint for navigating the impossible.

In our apartment, the kitchen, the stairwell, and even our rooms, we learned that a place could be more than it seemed; it could be a hub, a sanctuary, a workaround lab. From these small acts of ingenuity, I would later understand the truth my parents lived by: When the world confines you, the workarounds you invent can become lifelines.

CHAPTER 3

We learned how to sleep shallowly, ready for any emergency.

On September 22, 1980, I was four-and-a-half years old and on the cusp of primary school when the Iraqi Air Force launched surprise air strikes on ten Iranian airfields. The Iran-Iraq War began. Taking advantage of the turbulence in Iran after the Revolution and with the provocations of Ayatollah Khomeini against Iraq's Baath Party, while under the leadership of Saddam Hussein, Iraqi forces invaded and attacked the Iranian city of Khorramshahr. The war would last as long as my erratic primary school career—eight years.

Iraqi fighter jets launched missiles over Tehran, targeting civilian areas and ordinary citizens. When the warnings grew too frequent to trust—when Saddam Hussein's threats and the red sirens became a new part of the clockwork—we stopped tucking ourselves under the covers. The nights when our city would sink into total darkness as the government enforced blackouts to protect city centers from enemy planes, my parents instructed my sister and me to get under the beds.

My sister and I had twin-sized wood beds, small things with legs that sunk into the Persian rugs beneath. My parents shoved the heaviest objects they owned under those legs: my mother's medical textbooks—thick, black-backed tomes of anatomy and physiology, embryology, and pediatrics. Those books were the best hardbacks in the house; they were heavy enough to increase the gap between floor and mattress to a narrow, claustrophobic crawlspace. The books that made my mother a doctor—the very things that should have opened doors for her—became a literal prop for survival.

We made other makeshift defenses too. Windows were banded in tape in a net pattern or an X, so if glass shattered, the glass would (the theory went) cling together rather than become a rain of projectiles. Neighbors carried spare blankets and water jugs to each other. Someone learned the exact spot of the stairwell landing that was safest in our building. We rehearsed routes—bedroom to stairwell, stairwell to door—as if a choreography might save us from chaos.

Sleeping under a bed is not comfortable. It is narrow and awkward; the mattress won't fit beneath the frame, so you curl into ball or stuff a sleeping bag beneath, your knees bent, your blanket uncooperative. If a siren wailed, you woke, startled. One night, half-asleep under a bed, my mother's voice—"Let's go! To the stairwell!"—interrupted my dream. I shot up without remembering the low ceiling and struck my head on the underside of the bed. There was no time to rub the pain out. Disoriented, I felt my mother's hand—strong and immediately steadying—pulling me out of the dark. We went to bed fully clothed for these exact moments. When the sirens filled the air, there would be no time to dress, only enough to immediately vacate a place that was meant to be safe and sacred.

The logic of our protections lived partly in routine and partly in imagination. As a child, I tried to run scenarios: *How much air would be trapped if concrete fell? How long could a small space keep you alive before rescue?* Mostly, though, those anxious calculations were a way to feel some control. If you rehearsed damage, you could pretend to be prepared.

Sometimes the precautions saved us in small, practical ways. A few windows in our neighborhood, including in our home, did break one winter; families with taped panes woke to major cracks but no shattering or shards. We counted those moments as luck or validation of the workarounds we'd designed. Other times, when the warnings were false alarms—the Iraqi government threatening strikes to unsettle the economy—the city became a ghost town for a few days when a sea of cars drifted north to the Caspian Sea.

There were limits to what textbooks and masking tape could do. If a building were to collapse, a wooden bed supported by medical textbooks would be reduced to debris. As a child, I was not able to think about that; my hope and trust were boosted by naivete and inexperience. I learned that survival requires a community because I lived in moments watching my neighbors band together.

That improvisation seeped into everything else we did. If a law barred you from a university, you found a private tutor. If a job was closed to you because of your faith, you practiced your craft at home. Workarounds were small routes that let people live inside a system built to exclude them. The book-propped beds were only the first, literal, images of it.

I had seen that same logic in my mother's clinic-off-the-living-room, in our television hookup connected to our upstairs neighbor's satellite dish, and in the way neighbors pooled money and traded favors and information. Survival is rarely a single heroic act; it is a discipline born out of necessity.

When the sirens wailed, families would huddle as a community in the stairwell, holding on to each other as explosions cut through the night. The missiles' whirring reminded us of our vulnerability and made even brief attempts at sleep impossible.

I remember Mrs. Ghaffari, a neighbor from that era, who seemed to suffer from panic disorder. Each missile sent her into convulsions of hysteria, tears streaming freely down her cheeks. My father, ever the pragmatist, tried to console her: "If you hear explosions, it means you are still alive." I suspect this was partly a way for him to contain his own fear or a hope that I would overhear his rationale and find solace in it. On two separate occasions, missiles came close enough to shatter our windows. The vibration ran through the foundation of our home and is sometimes present in my body even today.

We tried to keep life as normal as possible during the war, even eating out once in a while at our local kabob house for special occasions—birthdays or my parents' anniversary. Dining out was rare and deeply cherished. Our house was near Vali-Asr Square, and several restaurants were within walking distance. One of them, located in Kabkanian alley, was a small, charming place called "Kabobi Sonnati" (Traditional Kabob House) at the corner of the street. Though the space was small, it was beautifully designed. It was inside a brick building, had a decorative oven rimmed with stones, and the smell of freshly baked lavash bread filled the air. It was clean, the owner was kind, and the food was delicious.

Before sunset, my sister, parents, and I would walk there. The scent of the kabob and bread would intoxicate us from blocks away. We'd order kabob and bread, steal the moist bread tucked beneath the kabob from one another, and enjoy the salad dressed with their signature house sauce—an orange-colored, sweet-and-sour delight that was one of the best. My mother even asked the owner for the recipe. I remember him saying, "Do you like our sauce, Doctor?" When my mother said yes, he replied, "Please come again; we'd be honored."

On the way back, walking home in the cold, I would shiver and ask my mom why I was shaking. She would explain that my blood had been redirected to my digestive system, and that next time, I should remember to bring my jacket. But each time, out of excitement, I would forget again—and the story would repeat itself.

In 1986, on a special occasion, we decided to return to Kabobi Sonnati. Full of childish joy, we set out. We ordered our usual dishes and the signature salad, but shortly after the food arrived, the power went out, and the horrifying air raid siren filled the room. The restaurant went dark. The only flickering light came from the gas oven. A deathly silence fell. Then we heard a voice:

"Attention! Attention! The signal you are hearing is a warning of danger or red alert. It means an aerial attack is imminent. Leave your workplace and proceed to the nearest shelter."

In the dark, my father rose and walked to the restaurant owner.

"Please bring us the check."

"Oh, it's nothing, Mr. Engineer."

"I insist. Please, hurry!"

"There's no rush, sir."

"I beg you. I don't want to die in debt. Let me die with a clear conscience."

It was a moment of normalcy intersecting with death—a lesson beyond the scope of the concerns my ten-year-old brain should've been handling. But instead, all the kids had to learn of the precariousness of life during wartime, where children became unintended witnesses to discussions of mortality.

My father paid the bill, even though the owner reminded him that if he were to die, they would all die together. We left our food uneaten. After hearing several deafening blasts—sounds of destruction and death in Tehran—we silently and coldly walked back home.

At school, "The Imposed War" became a frequent subject of conversation. Teachers used it as a springboard for lessons in geography, history, and morality. And to indoctrinate hatred toward "enemies."

Even amidst this chaos, my mother sought ways to maintain some semblance of normal childhood life for my sister and me. One such memory revolves around swimming lessons at a local apartment complex. Iran's strict gender segregation rules would not allow my sister to join the boys' lessons. No one at the pool knew her, so my mother gave my sister a boy's haircut and put a pair of boy's swim trunks on her with no top. That summer, we swam together like two "brothers," laughing and splashing freely. This act was our subtle rebellion, a small defiance against rigid societal norms.

Gender segregation extended far beyond swimming pools. Girls frequently had to dress as boys to attend sporting events or participate in activities deemed inappropriate for their sex. No matter how old you were, you could never speak to the opposite sex unless they were a close relative, which begged the question of how people ever met, got married, and procreated. Movies such as *Offside* illustrate the ongoing battle for access and equality, showing how deeply ingrained these restrictions remained decades after the revolution. Sahar Khodayari, the "Blue Girl," who self-immolated in 2019 after being barred from a soccer match, became a tragic emblem of these struggles. Even as these moments underscored the larger inequities of Iranian society under the Islamic Republic, my sister and I were fortunate to find small ways to subvert these rules. After all, we had learned from the best, the adults around us, setting an example of how will and spirit cannot be controlled, not truly.

Throughout the Iran–Iraq war, it was not just about fear, but how life kept going anyway. People still gathered. They still found ways to laugh. Even as a child, I could feel that these small moments were big deals. Every few weeks, my mother's friends met in someone's home. The doors would close, and everything changed. Music played. Women took off their scarves. There was food, laughter, even alcohol, and a kind of freedom I didn't see anywhere else.

One night, the host said there would be a surprise. An elderly woman walked in slowly, leaning on a cane. I didn't recognize her—but everyone else did. It was Delkash.

Before the revolution, she had been famous. Now she wasn't allowed to sing in public. But that night, she sat down and began to sing anyway. A piano joined her, then a drum. By the third song, everyone was singing along with her. I didn't know the songs, but I could feel something in the room shift, as if everyone had been holding a collective memory of culture and art, and now they could resurrect it together. Years later, I would understand what I was witnessing: the Islamic Republic thought it could steal people's souls by taking away their admiration of aesthetic beauty while silencing melodies. It sought not just to govern people's actions, but to redefine what they could hear, what they could celebrate, and ultimately, what they could remember. For my parents, their friends, and especially for Delkash, this wasn't just a party; it was something people needed to feel like themselves again. Soon after, Delkash passed away. Perhaps that living room performance had been her last.

* * *

Survival wasn't only about air raids and secret parties. It was also about a future that seemed to vanish before my eyes. As a Bahá'í in the Islamic Republic, the prospect of higher education was shut firmly in my face. University was not for us; ambition was a forbidden luxury. My father pulled me aside one evening and said, "If you can't study medicine, you must still have a skill. Something to keep you afloat." His solution was the Faraday Institute.

The name sounded like something scientific and modern, but the reality was a tired building where men in grease-stained shirts gathered after their day jobs. I was fifteen or sixteen, the youngest in the class by a decade, surrounded by bearded, gruff-looking men. They smoked, cursed softly, and tinkered with parts while I hovered in my seat, trying to keep up.

The evenings smelled of solder and metal shavings. The air hummed with the faint static of electricity, punctuated by the hiss of a hot iron touching wire. I learned how to read the spiderweb of electric circuits, how to isolate a faulty resistor, how to hold a soldering iron steady enough to reconnect a broken path. I learned about transistors and diodes and capacitors and managed to diagnose and replace the faulty parts. My hands smelled of chrome and copper when I rode the bus home.

Sometimes the practice became a skill. A family friend's radio broke, and I carried my tools to him, nervous. I opened the back, traced the problem, soldered a new connection, and when it crackled back to life, I felt a surge of pride; however, I knew this skill was not enough to sustain me for a lifetime. Another time, I repaired a television and earned a few dollars. In America, a broken television set meant buying a new one; in Iran, you made televisions last for twenty years if you could.

And in Iran, radios and televisions were more than appliances. They were lifelines. They carried news from beyond our borders, sometimes distorted but still invaluable. They carried pop songs and glimpses of forbidden worlds: women skating across ice in sequined costumes and couples kissing on screen—the kinds of sights the Islamic Republic insisted were "cultural invasion" and did not belong to us. These boxes of wires and glass were portals, and to fix one was to preserve a family's tenuous connection to hope.

Looking back, I see my father's wisdom. He hadn't suggested I learn to fix cars or air conditioners, trades that would have been practical but not what my heart called me to be. He steered me toward radios and televisions because they carried something more essential than comfort: They carried information. In a country where truth was a lie, where even education could be stolen from you, knowledge was the workaround. By learning to mend circuits, I wasn't just repairing machines; I was helping keep alive the possibility of connection.

From an early age, I learned improvisation came in many forms: finding ways to learn in a society that prohibited my religion, protecting myself during missile attacks, developing skills in case the only paths to higher education were closed to me, and, especially when it came to navigating the peculiarities of my own mind in a world determined to label it.

* * *

I was six years old when I first realized that my mind did not fit neatly into the boxes the world was organized into. Fridays in Iran were my equivalent of Sunday school: Bahá'í school. We gathered secretly in homes. Our volunteer teachers, usually young Bahá'í women, guided us through history, manners, and prayers. Memorization was expected. I hated memorization.

My mother, a pediatrician who could diagnose almost any ailment in a clinic, faced one of her greatest challenges at home: teaching me to memorize a simple prayer. One afternoon before departing to her home-based office, she stood in front of the bathroom mirror, fixing her hair with hairspray and a comb, the prayer book balanced on the glass shelf. I sat atop the toilet lid, attempting to repeat the words after her.

"O Son of Justice."

"Whither can a lover go?"

"But to the land of the beloved?"

I repeated each line, but when we circled back to the beginning, my memory failed as my brain fixated instead on her hair, her hairspray, and her image in the mirror. Mom's patience frayed. "What are you going to tell your teacher if you can't recite this prayer?" she demanded.

"I'll just tell the teacher nobody taught me this stuff," I said.

Her eyes narrowed. She lifted me from the toilet, leveled me with a glare, and spoke through clenched teeth about honesty. I sat frozen, as my mother grappled with the consequences of having a child who learned differently.

I didn't have a learning disability. I had ADHD, though nobody recognized it at the time. My mind refused to conform to rote memorization or rigid instruction, and the world labeled me mischievous or inattentive. My parents, concerned but confused by my obvious intellect and seeming unwillingness to participate in rote tasks, took me to a psychologist to better understand me and what my teachers had deemed defiance.

The psychologist administered IQ tests and other assessments. When the results came back, my parents were stunned: I had near genius-level intelligence. The same child who could not repeat a prayer without improvising, who seemed inattentive and insubordinate, was now officially recognized as exceptional.

"You will either be a very constructive, positive force in the world, or a force for negativity," the psychologist said, her face lit from below by the lamp on her desk. "You have the capacity for brilliance, but your choices will determine whether it is used for good or harm."

It was a binary choice I had never been offered before. I could rebel and resist, as I often did, or channel my mind in ways that could create, build, and contribute. Even then, I worried that the world I was living in might never allow me to exercise that potential freely. But I knew one thing. I was different, and I liked it.

I looked around me for proof that what made me different could be my power. If no one else would "get" me, I'd find other things to affirm who I was. One of the films we had on VHS in our Tehran apartment was *Funny Girl*, the Barbra Streisand musical with Omar Sharif. It was a love story and, most important to me, it was musical. I would sit at the piano, trying to figure out the scale in which she sang. Rewinding and replaying, I studied the phrasing, the emotion, the way her voice rose and fell. There she was, with her prominent nose and unconventional features, performing on stage, different from the classical ideal, and yet commanding the room. I revered her irreverence.

In the film, Barbra goes to audition at a prestigious venue—the Siegfried Follies, where professional artists regularly perform. She didn't have the classic show business looks or the stage presence the producer and director expected, yet she tried anyway. The scene has always stayed with me: She was well aware of her handicaps and chose to lean into them by entering the stage in roller skates, awkward and fearless, and began to sing. At first, the judges watch skeptically, uncertain. But as she performs, her talent and authenticity lead the way. At one point, aware of her unconventional appearance, she quips, "Is a nose with deviation such a crime against the nation?" The room chuckled, the tension dissolved, and she won them over. Could the inattentive, awkward-yet-self-aware kid win over those who play judge?

Even from war-torn Tehran in the 1980s, watching a 1964 film, I could feel the thrill of that moment. Here was proof that being different could be powerful, that audacity and individuality could create opportunity. Later in the movie, when Barbra's character goes off script during her first performance, improvising to engage the audience, the initially worried producers had no choice but to watch the magic unfold. The crowd laughed, applauded, and she triumphed.

I memorized the songs, sang along, and pieced together the story from context, since there were no subtitles. Every replay exposed me to English words, stretched my imagination, and gave me hope. In a household where movies were few and treasured, having our own copy meant I could watch and rewatch, letting every scene sink in. Streisand's defiance, her creativity, and her refusal to conform became more than entertainment—they were an early lesson in daring to be different and turning what others might see as limitation into an opportunity.

* * *

In June of 1989, Ayatollah Khomeini died. He was the founder of the Islamic Revolution—the man who had reshaped every corner of our lives. I was thirteen, in the middle of what should have been my final exams, but finals were postponed as the country paused to mourn—or at least to stage the mourning. On live television, the area where Khomeini was to be buried had been cleared and was packed with people waiting to witness his end.

I was hopeful; it was a new beginning.

I remember watching, glued to the screen, as the helicopter carrying his lifeless body hovered and disappeared, teasing the crowd below. The newscaster, caught up in the gravity of the moment, spoke of it as if the helicopter itself were a vessel of death. When the body finally arrived, wrapped in a shroud, the scene collapsed into chaos. People surged forward, trying to touch the shrouded body. Reverence, if it existed, dissolved into frenzy. Hands tore at the fabric, ripping the shroud to pieces, snatching fragments as if they carried blessing or fortune. And then the body itself was exposed—head and legs pointing in opposite directions, flung into disarray by the crowd.

My parents quickly turned off the television, shielding me from what they recognized as the grotesque spectacle of fanaticism. But I had seen, with the clarity only a child can have, that the emperor—so feared, so exalted—was nothing in death. And yet, tens of thousands of people had gathered, some out of devotion, others perhaps out of coercion or fear, all participating in this ritual of chaos. In that moment, I understood that the Islamic Republic was not a fleeting force. It was rooted in the minds and hearts of people who had bought into its ideology or were so afraid of it that they'd pretend to believe in something designed to hurt them. The regime was not fragile nor powerless; it was resilient, sustained by the unquestioning sycophants in the crowd.

My hope gave way to despair. Just a year before, the Iran-Iraq War had ended with a ceasefire, leaving the country exhausted and scarred. This was after the Ayatollah drank the "chalice of poison"—a reference to his acceptance of the terms of the United Nations Security Council Resolution 598. The Revolution had promised transformation, and perhaps I had believed that the death of a tyrant might usher in a new era. But Khomeini's funeral, chaotic and grotesque, proved otherwise. The man was gone, but the infrastructure he built was alive and well, ready to place a younger, equally hardline figure in power.

Watching it all unfold, I felt the first stirrings of learned helplessness. Through the crowd's behavior, I saw that so many Iranians were complicit in their own suffering. And I thought, *How can a kid like me become a doctor in a place so consumed by fear, obedience, and closed-mindedness?*

By the time Khomeini's body fell from the coffin and the crowd shredded the shroud, I understood that hoping for change and wishing on comets would not save me. I was officially disillusioned and no longer blind to the abuse of power and exploitation of devotion around me.

At home, the atmosphere was different. My father's world was quieter, more deliberate. In one corner of the room sat his little transistor radio—that portal to a forbidden universe. When the volume was low enough to avoid unwanted attention, foreign voices would emerge: BBC, Voice of America, stations crackling through static like distant beacons of light.

Prophet Muhammad, the founder of Islam, lay in a simple corner of a mosque in Medina, Saudi Arabia. People could visit, look at the modestly decorated enclosure, and pay their respects—but the tomb itself was humble, almost unassuming. And then there was the mausoleum built for Ayatollah Khomeini, south of Tehran, which was a spectacle of scale and opulence, dwarfing the resting place of the prophet himself. Even at thirteen, I could see the difference: This was not about reverence or religious observance. This was about power. The sheer size of the grand dome screamed authority and dominance. There was nowhere in the city you couldn't view it on a clear day from heights, a reminder of the Supreme Leader's watchful eye, no matter which leader lived at that time.

The Islamic Republic used architecture as propaganda. Khomeini, the man who had orchestrated so much misery—most notably the eight-year war with Iraq, leaving hundreds of thousands dead and countless others disabled or scarred psychologically—was now being immortalized in stone, marble, and gold. Resources that could have healed the nation, fed the hungry, or rebuilt what war had destroyed were poured into this monument, creating a structure bigger, more elaborate, more imposing than even the founder of the faith he claimed to serve.

It was a lesson I never forgot: Power, in the hands of the state, was masquerading as religion. The grandiosity of the mausoleum was meant to control, intimidate, and proclaim to the populace, "This is who we are. This is our might." Even at that age, I could see the cruelty in it.

CHAPTER 4

The streets of Tehran were always crowded, like Times Square or Broadway in New York, people walked shoulder to shoulder, and the crowd made it easier for people selling contraband to slip in and out of sight, just in case the regime had eyes on you. They were like vultures circling, until someone slipped up and was swooped off the street and into the back of a van.

That congestion offered a kind of cover. It made it easier for people selling bootleg cassettes, black-market jeans, and banned books to slip in and out of sight before the vultures' eyes could find them. But those eyes were everywhere. You learned early to assume you were being watched.

And always, there were sirens. Their wails cut through the city. They could mean anything: a car accident, a raid, an arrest. The instinct was to freeze, to step aside, to make way for something bigger, stronger, and in charge.

The danger was real. Every few blocks, there might've been a van parked at the curb or an ambulance weaving through traffic, siren off. But the "paramedics" weren't there to save anyone. They were agents—plainclothes members of the Islamic Republic's security forces who used those vehicles to blend in before making a move. One moment, you'd think someone was sick; the next, the back doors would fly open and men with guns and walkie talkies would rush into the crowd. They didn't announce themselves as police. Many times, they didn't even wear uniforms. To an outsider, it might have looked like a street fight breaking out, but if you looked closely, you could see the pistols at their belts.

They came for all kinds of reasons. Maybe a girl's headscarf had slipped too far back revealing her hair, maybe a boy was talking to a girl who wasn't his sister. Sometimes it was just bad luck—being in the wrong place when someone tipped off the morality police that young people were "fraternizing." You'd see a struggle, someone dragged into an unmarked van, the doors would slam shut—and that was that. Gone. You'd hope later they were just forced to sign some paper promising to behave, but you never knew.

I remember once during Ramadan, the month of fasting, I was walking down the street, minding my own business. I wasn't eating, wasn't drinking; I didn't even realize I was chewing gum.

Out of nowhere, I felt a sharp slap to the back of my neck. It sent me stumbling forward, arms flailing to keep from falling. Before I could turn around, a man in plain clothes grabbed me by the collar and bent me halfway forward. He marched me like that toward a trash can.

"Spit it out," he barked.

Terrified, I did.

"It's Ramadan," he said. "You're not allowed to do this."

And then he just let me go and vanished as suddenly as he had appeared.

To assert their authority, the Islamic Republic agents would never shy away from violence even if directed at minors. On another occasion, when, as teenagers, we were all riding in a friend's car to drive to a Chaharshanbeh Súri event where children and adults jump over a large fire a few days before Nowruz, the Persian New Year, our car was stopped by an agent on a motorcycle. Without any questioning or cause, he opened the rear passenger door and kicked his leg into the back seat. That kick landed on the left side of my chin and chipped my tooth. His reason? Boys and girls together in a car with loud music.

That uncertainty and the sense that at any moment you could be next, was the point. It kept people in line. You learned to read a crowd fast, to know which faces to trust, which to avoid. You learned to spot unmarked vans. And when one pulled up, even if you were doing nothing wrong, your stomach would tighten. Because in Tehran, the people meant to protect you weren't there to keep the peace. They were there to keep you afraid. And above it all, the sirens kept reminding you that danger had its own soundtrack. But even under that constant noise, people found ways to listen to what they loved. My parents included. With remarkable determination, they insisted on fighting for a small island of normalcy for my sister and me. Their chosen weapon was music.

After long deliberation, they decided we would take piano lessons. It was not a simple or safe decision. In those days, music was frowned upon by the Islamic Republic. Stories circulated—whispered from neighbor to neighbor—of musicians being cornered on the street, their instruments seized and smashed publicly by zealous revolutionaries who believed melody itself was a threat to their ideology. Carrying even a modest instrument outdoors could invite humiliation or violence.

But my parents, ever practical and quietly rebellious, found a solution. A piano, they reasoned, was too heavy to confiscate on the street. It anchored us—literally and figuratively—to our home. Teachers could come to us, or we could slip into a teacher's living room for lessons. In that simple decision, my parents gave us not just instruction in music, but an act of gentle defiance: a belief that beauty and the pursuit of arts still mattered.

Our small apartment occasionally transformed into a tiny concert hall. When relatives gathered, my sister and I would proudly showcase what we had learned. Someone would begin to hum, another would sing, and my grandmother—whose voice had a warmth that belonged to a different Iran—would often join in. Her singing filled the room with a kind of ancestral reassurance, as if reminding us that culture could survive anything.

Sometimes we visited other students' homes for makeshift recitals, families squeezing together on narrow sofas, applauding softly, nervously, but joyfully. Those evenings, however fragile, felt like stolen glimpses of a normal childhood.

My parents wanted the world of art to feel big, even when our world felt small. When an old slaughterhouse in South Tehran was transformed into a House of Culture, they embraced it eagerly. It was nearly an hour away from our home—an eternity in Tehran traffic—but they would buy tickets for performances so we could witness art on a real stage, under real lights. They wanted us to understand that creativity still existed in Iran, even if it had to survive underground, behind closed doors, or in the corners of repurposed buildings.

One evening my sister's piano teacher was scheduled to perform alongside an elderly percussionist at the House of Culture. We were thrilled, arriving early and full of anticipation. But at the entrance, the absurdity of the era confronted us yet again.

My mother, dressed modestly in pants and shoes, was refused entry because she wore no socks. Her ankles were showing.

Apparently, a few centimeters of a woman's skin posed a threat to the ideological purity of the revolutionaries guarding the door. So my parents stepped aside. Without hesitation, my father removed his own socks and handed them to my mother—because a man's ankles, it seemed, were not a source of national corruption.

We returned to the entrance. The guard looked at us suspiciously. My father, in a moment of quiet mockery, lifted the hem of his pants and exposed his now bare ankles.

"These are fine, right?" he asked.

The guard glared, then motioned us in with irritation. It was a small victory, but one that tasted sweeter for its pettiness. Inside, the atmosphere was no less tense. Revolutionary guards patrolled the aisles with flashlights, ready to shine bright beams into the faces of anyone who dared clap between pieces. Applause—something so instinctive, so human—was treated as an act of rebellion. Joy itself seemed forbidden, as though happiness were somehow anti-Islamic.

But people clapped anyway. Quietly at first, then louder. It was a fragile, trembling defiance, but a defiance nonetheless. When the lights finally dimmed and the curtains parted, I felt a rush of exhilaration. There stood my sister's teacher, poised at the piano beside an old man with his percussion instrument, the tombak—a mixture of Eastern and Western influences on one stage. The first notes filled the hall, and for a moment, the war, the fear, the restrictions—all of it receded. What remained was music. Pure. Unapologetic. Free.

That night stayed with me for decades. Perhaps I didn't realize it then, but something crystallized inside me—a conviction that art matters precisely because it *is* fragile, because it is vulnerable, because it is the first thing authoritarian systems try to silence. Those dimly lit rooms, those whispered recitals, those stolen applauses…they planted the seeds of what would one day become my life's work.

Years later, when I founded a nonprofit organization to support independent artists, I traced its origin back to these memories: to my grandmother's voice, to the piano in our living room, to the socks my father handed my mother at the entrance of a cultural hall, and to the glow of those flashlights searching the audience for signs of joy. In a world determined to suppress beauty, my parents taught us that creating and protecting beauty is an act of courage.

That lesson didn't stay abstract. It showed up in the smallest, most ordinary things—what we listened to, what we shared, what we risked loving out loud. Beauty wasn't just something you admired; it was something you had to *smuggle*, protect, and pass along quietly, as if it were contraband.

You couldn't buy Persian pop music in Iran after the Revolution. It was considered *haram*—un-Islamic, corrupting, and part of the so-called "cultural invasion." So, a black-market economy bloomed in the shadows, where music and movies traveled hand-to-hand, whispered into existence.

On certain afternoons, if you walked down Vali Asr Street—Tehran's main artery, always packed shoulder to shoulder like a parade—you could find it. You just had to know how to look. Among the crowds, young men leaned against the walls, arms crossed, one leg bent casually. They blended in with the noise of the city until you got close enough to hear them whisper, "New tapes…new cassettes." They sized you up before saying a word, checking your beard, your sleeves, your shoes. Were you the kind of man who prayed at the mosque or the kind who went to the gym in shorts and sneakers? A single glance told them who might crave the sounds of Los Angeles, the forbidden forum for Persian pop.

If they decided you were safe, the exchange began like a secret ritual. You'd nod, and one of them would murmur, "Who do you like? Hayedeh? Googoosh?" Hayedeh was the queen of exile, her voice deep and devastating, now living and recording in LA. "Yeah," you'd say, trying not to sound too eager, "Hayedeh." He'd also offer Western music such as Chris de Burgh, Modern Talking, or Samantha Fox.

He'd motion for you to follow him down a side street. You'd turn a corner, away from the crowd, to a quiet alley where a car sat parked as if it belonged to someone's home. He'd pop open the trunk. Inside, there were cassette cases stacked in a plastic bag. He'd pull one out, unmarked, unlabeled, and say the price.

The exchange was quick. He'd slip the tape into your hand. You'd toss the money directly into the trunk—he never carried the cash himself—and walk off in opposite directions as if you'd never met. Remaining cashless and cassetteless gave the peddler plausible deniability if he ever got caught.

Every part of the transaction had to look casual, because getting caught with Western or exile music could get you tossed into a van. These street dealers were psychologists as much as smugglers, reading faces, accents, and posture before whispering a single word.

For us, those cassettes were oxygen. They carried the sound of a free Iran—the one that existed only in Los Angeles recording studios, in an area dubbed "Tehrangeles," the heart of the Iranian diaspora.

Getting your hands on Western movies in 1980s Tehran was just as difficult. We had found a workaround for that. It was the same underground network that moved bootleg cassettes. Our source was a guy named Ashkan, or, as we called him, Action Ashkan. Every time he came by, he'd whisper like a spy at the door: "You want action? Romance? Drama?" He'd open his worn-out Samsonite briefcase like a magician revealing tricks. Most of the time the movie was action, because that's what sold—car chases, explosions, Stallone, Eastwood, Schwarzenegger. Occasionally, Ashkan would slip in a romance or a drama, like *Dances with Wolves*, which my whole family devoured. Every VHS tape was like hopping on the tail of a comet and transporting to another planet.

Of course, dealing with someone like Ashkan was risky. If a morality patrol showed up, both seller and buyer could be accused of cultural invasion and spreading "corruption on earth." Still, we waited for him eagerly. He'd show up every few weeks with his newest batch of tapes, and we'd gather around like gawkers. "Tonight, seven o'clock," he'd say. "Big American movie."

Before we had our own VCR, our neighbor had rigged up a splitter through the building's shared skylight—an actual coaxial cable snaking between apartments. When he played a tape on his VCR, everyone connected could watch it on their TVs. He'd call my father and say, "We're showing something tonight at eight. Tune to auxiliary channel." So, at exactly eight, our whole family would sit in front of the TV, waiting. If he paused the movie, we paused. "Maybe he's in the bathroom," my mother would say if we waited for too long. If it went past eight, my father would call him: "Mr. Z, are you still showing it?" And he'd say, "Sorry, a few minutes late. We're starting now."

When the movie finally came on, with its grainy picture and fuzzy sound, we'd sit there in awe. If there was a kissing scene, my mother would panic: "Close your eyes!" Sometimes the tape would stutter, or the neighbor would fast-forward through "inappropriate" scenes so quickly that the actors looked like they were dancing.

Later, when we finally got our own VCR, Ashkan became our direct line to the outside world. He'd come by quietly, hand us a black plastic bag, and disappear down the hall. If he labeled a movie family-friendly, we knew that was code for not family-friendly at all. Those were saved for after we went to bed.

We also had a Super 8 projector that kept us entertained. In the 1970s, owning one was a luxury—proof that you traveled, that you had seen places worth remembering. My father, always drawn to gadgets, had bought it on one of his trips abroad to see his brother in Austria. On certain evenings, my parents set it up in the living room. We didn't have a screen, so they aimed it at an off-white wall. The lights went out. The machine hummed to life.

There was no sound, just the click of the reel and the low whir of the fan. The speed was off, so people moved too fast, jerky and playful, like an old Charlie Chaplin film.

"That's your Aunt Nahid."

"That's my brother, Ezzat, in Austria."

Faces I knew only as names flickered past, appearing and disappearing before I could hold onto them. What stayed were the clothes. My mother, younger, wearing a bathing suit on a beach—abroad. Even swimming at the Caspian Sea, women were dressed from head to toe. It was a world I did not know. The projector became my quiet proof that another life had existed.

As the machine cooled down and the room darkened, I thought to myself, *Why do we live like this when life has so clearly been lived another way?*

* * *

In Iran, fall announced itself with the picking of pomegranates. They appeared everywhere—piled high at the markets, their skins a deep, leathery red. And with them came the ritual of my father at the kitchen table, seeding them with quiet concentration.

He was a master at it. Pomegranates are complicated fruits. They are stubborn, messy, and require patience to unlock their sweetness. In that way, they're like Iran itself: full of hidden richness, but you have to work hard to reach it. My father would spread out yesterday's newspaper across the table to catch the inevitable splatter of crimson juice. The sound of the seeds—arils, I later learned—hitting the metal bowl signaled success. By the end, my father's will was too much for the reluctant fruit, and the bowl would be full of ruby jewels.

We'd sprinkle them with salt and a dash of oregano, then dig in with spoons. Those same newspapers that caught the pomegranate juice had carried the stains of propaganda, the weight of the regime's stories. My father read them first, then put them to better use.

The arrival of pomegranates meant school was starting again. The air was cooler, the days shorter, and our hands, still sticky from fruit, would soon be holding pencils. Fall was the season of new notebooks, fresh uniforms, and always the same conflict of interest I had: reconciling my love for learning with the unfair rules and teachings of the Islamic Republic as it shaped a generation of what they called "tulips of the Revolution"—children born shortly before or during the Revolution, brainwashed by propaganda, especially against ideas of the West. A tulip is a beautiful flower—its three petals form a vibrant, wondrous chalice that captivates those who look on it. But there's another meaning hidden in the tulip—one we "tulips," proud to bear such a beautiful name, chose to overlook—the tulip is fleeting. That lovely chalice lasts only a few days before it withers, its petals fall, and its proud stem bows. For my generation, perhaps this meaning of the tulip was more fitting—for the hopes and beauties of our youth were replaced by the anxieties of war, death, coercion, and control.

The dismissal of Bahá'ís was felt everywhere in Iran, but nowhere more painfully than in schools. We weren't just unwanted; we were treated like refuse. Not human. Disposable. That word—refuse—has always stayed with me. Years later, when I read Emma Lazarus's poem "The New Colossus," the one engraved on the Statue of Liberty, I stopped at that line: "Give me your tired, your poor, your huddled masses yearning to breathe free…the wretched refuse of your teeming shore."

Lazarus knew exactly what she was doing when she chose that word. Refuse. Trash. Disposable. But she used it to transform meaning to say that what one land discards, another celebrates. That one person's trash could be another's treasure.

There's a word in Persian, *najis*, borrowed from Arabic, meaning "impure" or "untouchable." It's a word from Islamic jurisprudence used to describe those who don't belong or who are considered too dirty to touch. If a Bahá'í hand brushed a table, someone might wipe it down afterward. We were made to feel like najis. Like refuse.

Ronald Reagan announcing the big news that he was going to run for president said something that stuck with me and reminded me of my origin story: "In America, our origins matter less than our destinations." In Iran, your origins, whether religious or ethnic, defined your worth. America was a country that asked, "Where do you want to go?"

I was a Bahá'í, but I was also an American. One country's trash, another country's treasure—a treasure that only my small community and I would acknowledge. It became a challenge not to let the constant flood of others' disdain for you seep into your veins and corrupt your belief in yourself. Over time, with enough repetition, the regime's opinions could catch up to you if you were not supported by those who love you and honor your value. You might start believing your captors and equating their abuse with normalcy. My parents and my tight-knit Bahá'í community were committed to never letting that happen to one another, and especially not to their youth.

I got an early taste of that commitment when I was just seven years old and in the first grade. At the conclusion of the year, when my mother held my hand and walked me over to school to register me for the second grade, we were called into the principal's office. The principal, a tall, lanky man with a thick, unkempt beard meant to emanate piety, pointed to me and said, "Nowhere in Iran will I allow him to pursue an education." Then, with a smirk, he tore up each page in my academic file, tossing the pieces of my fledgling education across his desk and into the trash can.

"In fact, he will not be educated *anywhere*," he added with vitriol, trying to assert his power over my brief life. I was to be expelled immediately, despite reading and doing math beyond my years and having a perfect GPA as the top student in my class.

My mother, wearing her half-fastened hijab and knowing he was persecuting us for our Bahá'í faith, did not flinch. She wagged her finger at him and replied, "Those words are too big for your mouth, Mr. Principal."

Without my records, proving my academic achievements became impossible. But my mother had faced similar injustice before when she had marched out of her hospital administrator's office years earlier after being fired for her faith. It was no surprise that her son was being denied the same right to learn. We, the refuse, refused to stand down.

I began "school hopping," moving from headmaster to headmaster in search of a place that would allow *najis* to study. By the time I graduated eighth grade, I had attended three elementary schools, two middle schools, and two high schools. Each move reinforced the lesson that my parents and *Funny Girl* taught me: Nonconformity was a form of standing up for your uniqueness, especially in a society determined to impose sameness.

Imposition happened in many ways in the schools, including the use of corporal punishment. It became a normalized and accepted method of maintaining order and instilling discipline; an example that stands out clearly is when teachers would use corporal punishment against students for something as harmless as making and throwing paper planes in class.

Such incidents were far from unique. I recall a cleric who came to teach us Islamic studies; as soon as he entered, everyone stood up and recited a prayer, more out of respect than sincere devotion. Physical discipline in elementary school was expected when misbehaving or perceived disrespect occurred, reflecting broader societal attitudes regarding the raising and education of children. The cleric became indignant and brought two students to the front of the class and beat them before all the students as witnesses. "Did my clergy attire prompt you to recite a prayer? Do you do this for other teachers? Do you think I don't notice your ridicule?" These were the words he muttered as he used his arms and legs to show his rage to the entire classroom.

Despite this, I found it impossible to do things that were outside of my logic, and even as early as elementary school, my values didn't align with what was being imposed. This meant many calls home from school about my "disobedience" or "insubordination."

My father sat across from the headmaster, who adjusted his glasses nervously and cleared his throat.

"Mr. Missaghi," he began, "your son is not participating in our morning routine."

"My son?" my father said calmly. "What routine is that?"

"The slogans," the headmaster replied. "He refuses to repeat them."

My father raised an eyebrow. "What slogans?"

The headmaster hesitated, then said matter-of-factly: "We guide the children in saying, 'Death to America,' 'Death to Israel,' and others. He does not echo them. He only raises his fist."

My father smiled politely. "These are schoolchildren. Shouldn't you be promoting a culture of life rather than death?"

The headmaster blinked, unsure whether to be offended or embarrassed. "Well…this is what is expected. We cannot have students refusing to participate."

"So," my father continued, leaning forward, "you want children to begin their day by wishing death on entire nations? What purpose does that serve? What sort of hatred are you cultivating in them?"

The man looked flustered. "Sir, we don't create policy. We enforce it."

"I understand," my father said gently. "But consider what you're teaching them. This isn't Friday Prayer. Adults choose to attend those gatherings. These children are here for an education, not political theater."

The headmaster rubbed his forehead. "Regardless, he must fall in line. Please advise him of the expectations."

"I'll talk to him," my father said. "But he has his own opinions. And I hope you'll reconsider building a culture of death in your school."

And that was it. No threats. No follow-up demands. My father walked out calm, unbothered, as if this was just another absurdity he'd learned to navigate.

Later, he told me the whole conversation. He never insisted I comply. He only warned me, quietly, "They may dismiss you if you draw too much attention." He never told me to say things I didn't believe. That was against our family's entire worldview. Lip service was how others survived in that system—fake compliance for safety or advancement. But not us.

The slogans weren't the only way the regime tested us. I remember the large American flag they painted on the ground at the school entrance, forcing the children to walk over it every morning. I always sidestepped it, and sometimes administrators noticed. They didn't say anything at first. Eventually, though, they called my father in for that too.

"My son was born in the US," he told them. "How would you feel if your children were forced to stomp on your flag every day?"

They didn't argue. They just nodded, stiffly. And then, weeks later—without announcement, without explanation—the flag was quietly painted over and disappeared. Typical Islamic Republic: absolute enforcement followed by silent abandonment.

And through it all, in my childish logic, the whole spectacle felt ridiculous. I didn't want to wish death on anyone—not even a cockroach. And yet there we were, schoolchildren, expected to shout threats at foreign presidents whose names we barely knew. "Repeat this after me, so even Ronald Reagan can hear you and tremble: 'Death to America.'" And the student body strained its vocal cords in compliance before the school day began. It was indoctrination dressed as morning ritual. Performance disguised as patriotism. And from the very beginning, something in me simply refused to play along.

Right before I was kicked out of first grade to begin my school-hopping career, I sat in another stiff chair while the principal lectured me about why the Bahá'í Faith was not a religion but a "foreign invention" propagated by the British to create discord in Iranian society. His desk was cluttered with folders, a half-eaten apple, and an old cup of partially consumed tea. The blinds were drawn, as if secrecy added credibility.

"So," he said, leaning back, "you claim this…Bahá'í thing is a religion?"

"It is," I answered quietly.

"It is not." His voice was sharp. "It's a cult. Created by the British and the Zionists to divide Islamic societies. You are brainwashed."

I shook my head. "My family isn't British or Israeli. And we believe in God."

"You don't believe in God," he said mockingly. "And you have no scripture."

"We do," I insisted, my small voice trying to steady itself. "I can recite a prayer."

He raised an eyebrow. "A prayer? Fine. Show me."

I hesitated. "We don't pray sitting like this. We sit with our legs uncrossed, arms folded across our chest, and eyes closed. We pray in a posture of reverence."

Something in my tone, maybe the sincerity of it, amused him. "Very well," he said, shifting in his chair. "Show me."

He followed every instruction. Legs uncrossed. Hands across his chest. Eyes closed.

I closed mine too and began reciting the prayer.

After a few lines, he snapped, "Stop. Do you even know what that means?"

"I'm learning," I answered. "My Sunday School teacher said—"

"Who?" he cut in sharply. "Who teaches you this? Give me their address."

"I don't know the address," I said honestly. "But I can take you there. It's close to school."

That was apparently enough.

"Get your things," he ordered. "We're going now."

He held my hand as we left the school grounds; his grip was tight and his pace fast. I was too young to understand the inappropriateness of what was happening, but the moment did not feel right.

We had barely reached the corner when my father's car pulled up beside us. He rarely came to pick me up. Later, he would call it timing. Others might call it grace. He rolled down the window.

"Nizam?" he said, confused. "Why are you with the principal?"

Before I could answer, the principal spoke. "We're going to visit someone connected to his—"

"His what?" my father snapped.

He stepped out of the car, closing the door quietly behind him, the way he did when he was preparing to confront someone without causing a scene.

"My son will not be going anywhere with you," he said. "Not now, not ever. If you wish to speak with me, you can do it at the school. Not by dragging a seven-year-old through the streets."

The principal stiffened. "He's being taught nonsense. Lies. It's my responsibility to—"

"If you can't handle a seven-year-old's questions," my father interrupted calmly, "how are you supposed to handle adults? Or an entire school?"

The principal's face flushed.

"And one more thing," my father added. "You do not hold my son's hand. You do not take him anywhere without my permission. If you try this again, you won't be dealing with a child. You'll be dealing with me."

He opened the car door. "Nizam, get in."

I obeyed instantly.

As we pulled away, I saw the principal standing alone on the sidewalk, shrinking slowly into the distance.

Dad told my mother later that the principal accused them of "filling my mind with Bahá'í propaganda." My father just laughed and said, "If your ideology can be shaken by a child, the problem isn't the child."

That year was brutal, but I survived and finished at the top of my class. That didn't stop them from ripping up my transcripts and trying to keep me from going to any school in Tehran.

My mom spoke directly to my heart as she told me that this principal, just a man, could never determine my fate, and that we would find another way for me to learn. I remember wondering how we possibly could, now that I had no record of my first year in school.

But life had other plans. While that principal stood blocking one path, destiny placed Mr. Berenjian on the other side, holding a door open. Through sheer chance, my mom had a patient who was distantly related to him. He was the principal of another school, far from our home, but he offered hope when everything else felt hopeless.

Mr. Berenjian couldn't manufacture a transcript for me, but he gave me a challenge: if I could learn the entire second-grade curriculum over the summer and pass an exam, I could skip directly into third grade at his school. I accepted immediately. Other kids played in the streets; I hit the books. My parents hired a tutor named Ziba to help me.

Ziba was an incredible teacher who had lost her job for being a Bahá'í. Every day, she drilled me, pushed me, encouraged me, and prepared me for the exam. And guess what? I aced it. Not only did I make it to third grade; I breezed right in.

Mr. Berenjian wasn't a Bahá'í himself, but he believed in education for everyone, regardless of background. He stood up when others sat down. Seeing an eager student, he opened the doors wide and accepted the potential cost of that decision if it were ever discovered by the Islamic Republic authorities.

He became an early stamp in my metaphorical passport—someone who stepped in, upheld me, and helped move my life forward when the official paths were closed. And doors seemed to keep closing, especially when it came to school.

I was about eleven or twelve—just starting middle school—on the day we went to the Ministry of Education to protest another unfair dismissal. At first my dad seemed calm as we sat across from the official, his hands resting casually on the glass table. But everything shifted the moment he mentioned we were Bahá'ís, the *najis,* "unclean." The man exploded to his feet and barked, "Don't touch my table."

My dad tried to assert our rights as citizens, pointing out that those rights were protected by the Constitution. The official sneered, "The Constitution is written for humans," implying we were something less. Before we could process that, he added, "I thirst for your blood."

Silence followed. Then my father did something I will never forget. Pointing to his own jugular, he said, "Here. Cut it. Drink it, if it helps you feel better." His voice was steady, but his eyes were burning.

Two guards rushed in, gently taking my dad by the arms and saying, "Sir, it appears you are upset; please control yourself," before escorting him out.

It wasn't just the threat or the dismissal that stayed with me; it was the realization of how deep the prejudice ran. That day wasn't only about my education; it revealed a hostility so intense that an official would talk openly, without consequence, of thirsting for our blood. As I flinched in fear, my parents knew he and many of the people in charge were merely pretending to be better than us. What struck me most wasn't just what they said, but how they looked. They all seemed to follow the same pattern—rings with colored stones, untrimmed beards, serious voices that made them sound important. But what drew my eyes every time was the mark on their foreheads—dark, sometimes thick, almost scabbed over, like a wound that had decided to stay. The larger it was, the more it seemed to speak for them, a shorthand signal that demanded they not be questioned or disobeyed.

I later learned the mark came from prayer—from the prostrating, pressing the forehead down again and again, often against a small stone. Over time, the skin could darken. But even as a child, I noticed something didn't add up. Some of the kindest, most religious people I knew had no such mark on their foreheads at all. And some of the men whose foreheads looked the most worn—almost forced—were the ones who frightened me the most. Sometimes what was meant to show devotion looked more like something else entirely—disdain, prejudice, and even thirst for blood.

My father faced that hatred with unwavering courage. He didn't cower; he once again exposed the absurdity of their cruelty. The experience terrified me, but it taught me something essential: the importance of standing up for what is right, even when fear grips you.

CHAPTER 5

In the fall of 1989, I enrolled in a high school named The Tulips of the Revolution. As I approached the entrance, I noticed the red, white, and blue colors of the American flag painted on the concrete where the doors were jammed open. Instead of fifty white stars, fifty white skulls were meticulously painted. The mural was so large it was impossible to enter the school without stepping on the flag—a symbolic demonstration of allegiance to the Islamic Republic and disdain toward the "Great Satan," as America was often called by the Islamic Republic authorities. Stepping on it wasn't just symbolic; this act demonstrated our devotion and potential hatred toward our collective and unseen enemy.

I didn't share with many peers that this enemy of theirs was also my homeland, a place that didn't know me at all, and yet, by mark of my birth, valued me enough to give me paperwork that the Iranian government wouldn't.

I'd been defying the tulip teachings since I was seven, but the flag was still the universal test we all had to pass. No matter how rebellious you thought you were, every tulip arrived at high school with the same baseline expectation stamped onto them.

As a kid, I used to moonwalk in the living room and pretend I was Michael Jackson, wishing the sidewalk would light up under my feet like in *Billie Jean*. Now, instead of glowing pavement, I was being forced to step on a field of painted skulls and state-sanctioned vitriol. I slowed as I neared the flag. The weight of history pressed down on me, along with the eyes of teachers and classmates who had already made their choice. My heart thudded in my ears.

I stepped to the edge of the painted stripes and, balancing carefully, tiptoed along the narrow border, inching my way to the entrance without letting my feet touch the skull-lined field of blue. I nearly lost my balance, but I kept going, refusing to give them the satisfaction of a misstep.

I was immediately reprimanded, labeled a troublemaker, and subjected to increased scrutiny. Yet the emotional repercussions far outweighed any punishment: This act served as an expression of my beliefs. I had stood against oppression and showed my commitment to upholding ideals represented by the American flag. I reasoned with the curious administrator that, all politics aside, much in the same way that we as a people would find it objectionable for American schoolchildren to walk on an Iranian flag, an entire people would find this flag and its placement distasteful.

Coming of age for a teenager is riddled with confusion, angst, and uncertainty. Coming of age in Iran was marked by moments like this one, where choice and consequence were always at odds. The more experiences I had, the more it was revealed to me that even the simplest pleasures would be difficult.

Could I live like this forever?

It didn't matter that my latest IQ score indicated I was at the border of genius level or that thousands of other young scholars were being denied access to higher education; the regime did not want to benefit from our gifts and talents. They simply wished to have a homogenous young population that adhered to their beliefs and followed marching orders.

The hope and wonder I had let Halley's Comet blaze for me was quickly fizzling out. Instead of wondering what kind of future Halley would carry back to me, I began to dream about leaving. Escape at first was only a thought experiment, as I looked to nature, music, science, and friendships to provide a sense of normalcy in a world I was now old enough to realize was far from "normal."

* * *

I tightened the striped laces of my running shoes and caught up to my friends. The white soles were as bright and smooth as the no-name shoebox I had recently pulled the sneakers from. On this hike, I'd scuff up the leather; break in the heels.

As teens, my Bahá'í friends and I had made the hiking trails of the southern Alborz mountain range, just north of Tehran, our place to breathe. The loose translation of Alborz is "mountain rampart." A rampart is a castle wall or a walled city. But it was back in our hometown of Tehran where we felt our walls closing in—where watchtowers of authorities stood, waiting to catch us in acts associated with the infidel.

On weekends, we'd alternate between leisurely escapades and more strenuous paths. I never felt like I walked the same trail twice, always spotting a new gift of nature—alley-gardens with tall trees that opened as umbrellas of shade; a sea of wild cypress and olive trees that parted to reveal ancient houses with patinaed doors; and in the silky sky, soaring eagles with wingspans as wide as freedom itself.

Also, there were vultures.

The narrower the valley, the better the acoustics between two mountains. We'd yodel and catch our echoes like boomerangs, delighted by the powerful vibrations of our voices. Our friend with a musical background was often possessed to crane his neck to the sky and sing. His classically trained vibrato took us on a joyride along the peaks and valleys of his song, around which the vultures circled. Plain-clothed agents of the Regime often patrolled the trails—morality police who hovered until someone did something out of step with the strict codes of the Islamic Republic.

For the more arduous hikes, I'd clip my Sony Walkman to my waistband and place the cushioned headphones over my ears like two sponges soaking up the sounds in my head. Endless thoughts and concerns and questions about my future raged into noise, but once my cassette was popped into place and the reels began to turn like the wheels of a locomotive, my Persian dance music took me away.

We set our things on a flat rock near the water—towels, clothes, bags, and the radio—before we jumped in. We were in our bathing suits, laughing, splashing around, not thinking about anything except how cold the stream was. When the music stopped, I assumed the cassette had finished. But when we walked back to the rock, everything was there except the radio. Just the radio.

My stomach dropped. This wasn't some random cassette player. This was the Austrian radio—the one my dad had treasured for years, a gift from his brother, carried across borders and life's milestones. It was the radio he used to listen to the news through all the *parazit*—the static and deliberate interference the government pumped into foreign broadcasts. That radio had been his lifeline to a world beyond Iran. And I had brought it on a hike.

I remember thinking, *This is catastrophic. He loves that radio. He listens to the news on that radio.* I couldn't imagine him discovering it was gone.

My friend Babak was with me, and after watching me fall apart for a minute, he said, almost casually, "You know...my grandpa has the exact same one." His grandpa lived in a town outside Tehran. I stared at him like he'd just handed me oxygen. "Please," I said. "I need to buy it...whatever it costs."

I scraped together every bit of money I had. The old man was more than happy to part with the radio—too happy, really—and Babak likely pocketed the cash. I didn't care. All I cared about was replacing it before my dad realized his treasured radio had disappeared forever.

When I got home, I placed the replica in its usual spot, as if nothing had happened. To this day, my dad has no idea that the original radio was stolen on a hike.

I never found out who took it. Maybe other hikers who spotted a nice radio with a cassette player. Maybe one of those rangers who policed music on the trails and decided it wasn't "Islamic enough." I'll never know. But everything else we'd left on that rock stayed untouched.

The thing about those years was that even with all the pressure around us, even while the country tried to make us small, we still somehow managed to be kids. Regular, fun-loving kids, finding ways to express ourselves beyond what the state had intended us to be—withering tulips.

The regime believed we were the kids whose minds could be molded from the very beginning into perfect ideological citizens. The idea was to start early enough so the system could shape our thoughts, our loyalties, even our worldview. If the state controlled what we saw, heard, and learned—children's programming, school rituals, textbooks, the morning slogans—then an entire generation could be raised in perfect ideological uniformity. A nation grown from a single seed of mind control.

The regime wasn't subtle about their intentions. It openly celebrated the creation of this new "revolutionary" generation, the children who would carry the ideals of the Islamic Republic forward long after the original revolutionaries were gone.

In fact, the high school I attended was literally named after this concept: Tulips of the Revolution High School. What the regime didn't anticipate, however, was that many of us grew up resenting the manipulation. My classmates especially had open disdain for the people—teachers, administrators, media producers—who tried so hard to manage every aspect of our thinking. The more they pushed, the more resistance they created. Not open rebellion—no one was stupid enough for that—but quiet, constant refusal. Humor. Sarcasm. Eye rolls. Selective hearing.

There was even a joke we used among ourselves. In Persian, "tulips of the revolution"—*Lalehā-ye Enqelāb*, rhymes closely with the phrase for sewage pipes—*Lúleha-ye Fazeláb*. The two sound similar enough that you could swap one for the other under your breath. So whenever the officials would proudly refer to us as the "tulips of the revolution," some kids would snicker, whispering: "You mean the sewage pipes?"

In high school, my friends and I had convinced ourselves we were great rebels—bold nonconformists. And how did we express that revolutionary spirit? By making fun of our teachers. Of course.

We still had the old blackboards, so every lesson was a chalk-dust desert. Our math teachers would attack the board with such intensity that you could taste the white powder from the cloud above them. We decided to add to the atmosphere.

The second a teacher turned his back to create a chalk-dust monsoon of math tables and proofs, we'd burp out bizarre animal noises, squeaks, honks, and whispered nonsense syllables. We burned incense that smelled like a barn. We engineered paper airplanes and flung them at the back of the heads of our earnest educators, then sat there, innocent and wide-eyed with our pencils furiously scribbling the moment the teacher turned around. On another occasion, when the school had asked each class to appoint a task force to decorate the classroom for the anniversary of the Islamic Revolution, my classmates, who clearly saw no cause for such celebration, chose to inflate condoms instead of balloons and taped them along with ribbons to the windows and the ceiling. When Mr. Seifi, the administrator, walked in with a stern face and inquired who had done the decorations, the class fell silent. He looked at the "decorations" and could not contain himself. He let out a chuckle, and the class exploded in laughter. With his anger dissipated, he spoke softly, "Please remove these because *we* will all be in trouble otherwise."

We were absolute menaces, turning arithmetic into anarchy, or our version of it anyway.

And then there was poor Mr. Hoghoughi, our geometry teacher, the prime target of our idiocy. He had a slight limp, and one of his eyes drifted a bit, giving him an unintentionally dramatic look—as if he were trying to monitor two parallel universes at once. He would blaze through the lesson in thirty or forty minutes, then ease himself into a seat, put his feet up on the front bench, and say with deep apology: "Gentlemen…I'm very sorry. I have varicose veins."

He was teaching us through pain every day. And what did we do? We mimicked his limp, crossed our eyes, put our legs up, and gave fake geometry lectures in his exact tone. I once tried to imitate his walk and his eyes simultaneously and nearly collided with the chalkboard. It was pure cruelty disguised as comedy—and we thought we were brilliant.

When we were studying for our college entrance exams—the equivalent of SAT prep—there was one geometry book that everyone swore by. We sat around flipping through it when someone said, "Guys…look at the author."

There at the top of the page, in clean, confident print: Mr. Hoghoughi.

While we were busy mockingly crossing our eyes and limping, he was literally shaping the national curriculum. I remember staring at his name, feeling a hot wave of guilt and humiliation wash over me. We hadn't just made fun of a tired teacher. We had mocked a quiet genius who was probably dragging himself to school each day because he had a family to support.

But that's who we were then: immature, chaotic, defiant kids trying to be normal teenagers in a place that made normality nearly impossible. And sometimes, that meant the joke—deservedly—was on us.

The thrill of testing the rules, even just a little, became a kind of education in its own right. It was in this spirit of risk and discovery that I found myself one warm, muggy evening making my way, with my loyal friend Babak, to a clandestine co-ed party thrown for a classmate accepted into medical school. Fear and excitement churned inside me. Being caught could mean serious trouble—or worse—but the need for freedom outweighed any risk.

Music and laughter spilled from the house the moment I arrived, intoxicating in every sense. For a few hours, we forgot the oppressive world outside, dancing, joking, and simply being ourselves while trying to impress the girls in attendance. But the thrill was always tempered by the knowledge that at any moment, it could all come crashing down.

Then the sirens came. Panic erupted. Everyone scrambled. My heart pounded. The main door was too risky, so I dove for a small window at the back, squeezing through into the night. Fresh air hit my face as adrenaline surged and my body shivered, and I ran through a dimly lit alley, every shadow a potential officer.

The streets were mostly empty. After what felt like forever, I reached a familiar corner and spotted a store just closing. I explained my predicament to the puzzled owner as I asked for some money for a taxi since I left my wallet and jacket behind. I offered my watch as collateral, and he agreed to drive me home, warning me of the authorities' ruthlessness along the way.

By midnight, I was back in our alley, my heart still racing. I rang the doorbell to Babak's residence and his parents emerged in their pajamas. I told them about the sneak-out and shared that their son was likely detained. His father quickly dressed to see if he could retrieve him. I pleaded with them to keep my presence a secret from my own parents, who had warned me not to go to such parties to avoid drawing attention to our family. I slipped quietly into my mother's office, so they wouldn't hear me sneak back into the house. I collapsed onto the examining table, my mind spinning with worry for my friends and the danger we all faced simply for chasing a moment of youthful normalcy.

Babak had to spend the night in detention, and his father was denied access to him that evening. Upon returning, his father paid a fine and Babak had to sign an attestation that he would never participate in such parties along with a written acknowledgment that he now had a record with a stern warning that would compound any future "moral infractions."

That night was another rehearsal in the lifelong performance we were expected to master: the split between who you were at home and who you could be outside. Most Iranians would recognize this instinctively. The lack of continuity—of being unable to exist as one's whole self—creates a quiet identity crisis. You learn quickly that survival depends on reading a room, knowing exactly *who* you can say *what* to and when silence is safer than truth.

It was the same skill required of the men who sold contraband cassettes on street corners. They had to scan faces, listen for tone, intuit values—decide in seconds whose home life might align with theirs and whose curiosity might turn into danger.

Later, we learned that many of the revolution's architects lived double lives not unlike ours—only better hidden. Years afterward, when leaked footage surfaced of Ali Shamkhani's daughter's wedding, we watched as the bride wore a plunging neckline and Shamkhani's wife appeared without a head covering. The rules, it turned out, were elastic for those in power. Duplicity wasn't a flaw of the system. It *was* the system.

* * *

My friends who were not Bahá'í never quite knew what to make of me, my family's customs, or the Bahá'í faith itself. Everything

I did seemed to be viewed through the lens of being different. Even the simplest things could turn into cultural curiosities.

I remember one weekend in high school when a friend came over to study. My mother, ever the gracious host, noticed we'd been working for a while and decided to bring us something refreshing. She started with freshly pressed carrot juice, then a little later brought orange juice, and then, as the afternoon wore on, some sort of berry smoothie she'd blended from leftover fruit in the fridge.

By the third glass, my friend looked at me wide-eyed and said, "So…is this the Bahá'í Festival of Juicing?"

I blinked. "What?"

He said, "I don't know! I've never had this much juice in one day. I figured it must be some kind of religious thing you guys do!"

We both burst out laughing, but inside, I realized how even small things could get filtered through the perception of my being "other." Even my mother just making sure a couple of teenagers were hydrated became exotic, turned into a "Bahá'í ritual."

It wasn't meant maliciously, of course. My friend was genuinely trying to make sense of our world, to fit it into his frame of understanding. But that moment stayed with me—how easily ordinary things could be misunderstood when viewed through the lens of difference.

And maybe that's why we clung so tightly to the places where we *didn't* have to explain ourselves. We still managed to build something that felt like a real life, celebrating what made us different—full of movement, humor, travel, and each other. One of the most important lifelines we had were the Bahá'í youth camps and weekend gatherings. If you were lucky in our community, you grew up with mixers, teen groups, and junior youth groups—little ecosystems of freedom in a world that tried to deny it to us.

Boys and girls were together. Nobody was covered. Nobody policed our every move except for adult chaperones who had volunteered their time to be present. Local families would charter a minibus, pile a bunch of us in, and take us out of Tehran to someone's *bagh*—a "garden," which usually meant a modest chalet on a big piece of land, sometimes even with a river running through it. We'd spend the whole weekend there. Someone always had a guitar. Someone always started singing, and the rest of us would join in the chorus. Another would play the goblet drum—the *tombak*—which made dancing irresistible. Music and laughter folded into the landscape like it had been waiting for us.

Before any of the fun, though, there was always the devotional. We'd sit together in silence, offer prayers, and then everyone would introduce themselves—especially when the youth of two districts of Tehran, like three and six, mixed together. You'd arrive not knowing half the faces and leave wondering how you ever lived without them.

After that, it was pure, spontaneous joy. Ping-pong tournaments that erupted out of nowhere. Dancing. Wrestling. Pillow fights. People tumbling into a laughing heap after someone lost their balance. The kind of physical closeness that was natural to us but forbidden everywhere else. We didn't think in categories of "boys" and "girls." We were just youth—alive, energetic, and completely ourselves.

There's a photo somewhere of all of us jammed onto a couch. One of the girls couldn't fit in the frame, so she just stretched herself across our laps, grinning. In Iran, where boys and girls weren't supposed to even look at each other in public, we socialized inside the Bahá'í community, and it felt like a small pocket of air in a suffocating room.

Looking back, I think the adults understood exactly what was at stake. They didn't create these gatherings only so we could socialize; they created them so we wouldn't drift away. To stay Bahá'í meant accepting real risks and walking away from certain opportunities. The least they could give us was belonging—something beautiful enough that no form we could fill out, no promise of safety, could easily pull us away from.

As my friends and I grew older, our families became even more intentional about connecting us to one another and to a version of Iran that was bigger, freer, and more beautiful than what the regime wanted us to see. Our parents understood—often more clearly than we did—that an entire generation was being targeted for indoctrination. They refused to let that happen quietly.

They had lived through *another* Iran, one where joy, music, free agency, and critical thought weren't suspicious. They wanted us to know that version too—not as nostalgia, but as inheritance. They told stories of the "good old days," of how Iran *was*, how America *was*, and what freedom looked like in practice. Not because they were naïve, but because they knew we needed a counter-narrative to survive psychologically.

Part of the reason, too, was that—early on—many Iranian families believed the new regime was temporary. People waited for a coup, an overthrow, some correction that never came. Instead, the system consolidated, eliminated its own early supporters, and hardened into a theocracy that reached into every corner of life: how to think, how to behave, how to believe.

So our parents doubled down. They taught us to question. They wanted us to grow up knowing: *This is not normal.*

Humor became one of their tools. Iranians have long used jokes as a coping mechanism, and during gatherings, my father was the unofficial entertainer. He had an encyclopedic memory and an impeccable sense of timing. Someone would always turn to him and say, "Okay, time for jokes." And off he went—accent work, punchlines, everything. Many of the jokes were political, ridiculing high-ranking clerics who all had pseudonyms like "the deceptive cat." Everyone knew who was who.

His humor would also be ever present in family gatherings to diffuse any tension. When I was six years old in 1982, my grandmother, Monir Khanum—the luminous lady—was over for lunch. I sat quietly, half-listening to the adults' conversation, not fully grasping the weight of their words. My grandmother, frail with age and health troubles, brought up something that lingered with me long after: the Bahá'í cemetery in Tehran, Golestan-e Javid, had been confiscated and bulldozed by the Islamic Republic authorities. This is where her own father and her late husband had been buried. Tehran's Bahá'í cemetery was gone without a trace. Outside of the toll of not being able to visit her family's graveyards any longer, she feared what would become of her when her time came, since the Islamic Republic barred Bahá'ís from Muslim cemeteries and left the community with no burial ground.

After an uncomfortable silence, my father, with a playful grin, said, "Well, Monir Khanum, I guess that means you'll have to live forever!" Everyone laughed, but beneath the laughter was a quiet defiance I could feel. Then, with a twinkle in his eye, my father added, "Did you know the Bahá'í administration issued a letter about this? They said no member of the community is allowed to die until the cemetery situation is resolved!"

For a moment, his words seemed an oddly comforting solution, until my grandmother smiled knowingly and said, "You're pulling my leg, aren't you?" We all laughed, but even as a child, I sensed the gravity. It struck me then—how terrible it was that even in death, the Bahá'í families were denied peace.

Humor was a defense mechanism against danger, but could invite danger itself. If a child repeated the same jokes at school—and children always repeat what adults think they won't—the authorities could trace the sentiment back to the household. So, my parents sat me down and said, "These jokes stay at home. Not even with friends." They were teaching us boundaries, but also the idea that questioning authority—even through humor—was natural and necessary.

Those lessons in critical thinking, subtle rebellion, and cultural preservation infused all the ways they raised us, including the way we traveled.

It was during one of our many trips to the Caspian Sea—those makeshift family caravans we preferred over organized tours—that I felt the power of these counter-narratives most vividly. Two or three cars packed with relatives and close friends, coolers wedged between feet, someone always singing off-key. The drives north were their own kind of adventure. Each mile brought the feeling that freedom lived somewhere just beyond the mountains.

These Caspian Sea trips were an annual tradition I waited for with almost impatient excitement. After long days of swimming and playing on the shore, we returned to our villa hungry and sunburned. Dinner would be spread on the floor to fit everyone—platters of rice, stews, fresh herbs. Someone always had a cassette of banned pop music. We'd listen quietly at first, then less quietly. Later we'd wander through the garden, picking fruit, looking for snails or frogs, soaking in a world that felt untouched by politics.

Those summers tethered us to one another. They carved out a sanctuary where family, nature, and culture could thrive despite everything happening outside.

Travel inside Iran became a kind of education. Because we weren't allowed to leave the country, my family explored it deeply—its history, its artistry, its ancient bones. Many of my happiest childhood memories come from these trips rather than from routine school days.

We visited Esfahan—"Half of the World"—with its mosques tiled like galaxies and its celebrated bridges where locals sang into the arches. Kashan, with its gardens and historic homes, was special to us not only for its beauty but because it was our ancestral city—where my great-grandfather Nizam lived, and where my maternal great-uncle, Dr. Sulayman Berjis, had been brutally murdered by zealots.

We explored Yazd's adobe alleys, its windcatchers, its Zoroastrian Fire Temple, and Towers of Silence. Kerman enchanted us with the Ganjali Khan Complex, Shazdeh Garden, and the vast, otherworldly Lut Desert. We saw the Citadel of Bam long before the 2003 earthquake devastated it.

Tabriz was another favorite with its Blue Mosque, bazaars, and parks. In Urmia we tasted food with Turkish influence and marveled at the salt lake that has since shrunk dramatically to a salt field due to mismanagement by the Regime. We took turns in the natural hot springs, women's shift then men's, each of us returning pink-skinned and relaxed.

Over and over, these places taught us who we were—not according to the regime, but according to history, culture, and memory.

We also joined organized tours, usually to historical cities. The bus rides themselves became events. Packed with families, we would wait until we crossed the city limits. Then, like clockwork, curtains closed, hijabs slipped off, forbidden pop music blasted through small speakers, and people danced in the aisles as the bus bounced along rural roads.

Soon someone would pick up the bullhorn and tell jokes. The bus would erupt in laughter, bodies swaying, hair uncovered, music illegal but joyous.

CHAPTER 6

As I neared the completion of high school, it was as if I had an internal clock ticking away at my educational opportunities that became increasingly hard to ignore. Despite my academic achievements and unwavering determination, belonging to the Bahá'í faith meant that higher education opportunities in Iran were barred to me.

The exclusion took many forms. The most common was that the registration for the national college admissions test would exclude the Bahá'í applicants by denying them entrance permits. Another method was to permit the Bahá'í students to take the test; however, during enrollment, they would be marked as having incomplete files without any opportunity to complete the process. Yet another method was to permit enrollment into a university and, after a few semesters, an asterisk was placed next to the student's name in the computer system, which effectively stripped the Bahá'í students of their rights as university attendees, making registration, viewing grades, or ordering transcripts impossible, banning them from higher education for life.

As I watched my high school classmates prepare for the university admissions exam, I remember feeling helpless as they studied hard for their tests. I had once been hopeful that by the time it was my turn to pursue higher education, this injustice would end, but those days seemed galaxies away.

I went to pick up my registration card for the admissions test with Babak. He went first. The administrator flipped through the cards. "Ah, here's yours," he said, handing one to Babak.

I stepped forward. "My last name is…"

He flipped through the cards again. And again. He squinted at the spelling. "Are you sure this is correct?"

"Yes," I said, handing him the confirmation number I'd received in the mail.

He took it, stood up, and leaned close, his voice on the down low. "Are you…a religious minority?"

"Yes," I stated firmly. "But I am also an Iranian citizen, and the Constitution guarantees my right to an education."

He stared at me, expressionless. "I am just…following orders."

As my final year of high school progressed, anxiety filled the air. While my classmates prepared for university entrance exams, I grappled with the reality that I wouldn't even be allowed to take them. I would have to serve in the military for two years right after high school, since I could not get a student exemption.

Without university as an option, this meant my only option was agreeing to the two-year stint; the thought of serving an institution that did not recognize my basic human rights was unbearable for me. *Why would anyone serve a country that refuses to serve them in return?*

Without an official discharge paper from military service, finding work was nearly impossible. Employers required proof to hire you; without it, you were out of luck.

Society was placing me under immense strain. Conversations with Muslim friends left them confused as to why I was trying to avoid military service so desperately. For them, it was an inevitable part of growing up. They couldn't comprehend all the layers of fear and discrimination I would face as an outcast in a military service environment, which included systemic bias against Bahá'ís within its ranks and abuse from those serving.

Many Bahá'ís found that leaving Iran was their only viable option, so families pooled together savings to send their sons and daughters overseas in hopes that they might find sanctuary somewhere that allowed them to pursue their goals freely. But this was like playing Russian roulette with young lives.

We had all heard about one of my father's close friends whose son, Payam Pakzad, had been smuggled out of Iran into Turkey. I still emphasize his name because if you look him up today, you'll see who he became. Berkeley. Caltech. Multiple peer reviewed articles. And now, I believe, Google. A mind like that should have been a national treasure. Instead, he was refuse.

Payam was known as the boy genius. He competed in Iran's Olympiad and ranked first in physics. He was supposed to represent Iran internationally that year, in Holland. He even boarded the plane. And then an agent of the Islamic Republic pulled him off. He just walked onto the aircraft and removed him. Why? Because he was a Bahá'í. They didn't want a Bahá'í bringing honor to Iran.

He was sent home. A reserve student was sent in his place despite Payam having the highest score of the five-member team.

Normally, anyone who ranked that highly in Olympiad competitions didn't need to take the Iranian equivalent of the SAT. It warranted an automatic university admission at the institution of his choice. But when Payam tried to use that rule, they told him no. "You're Bahá'í. You don't get to go."

His parents were desperate. Their son wasn't just bright; he was one of the brightest people anyone had ever met. He needed a future, and he wasn't going to find it in Iran. So they found a smuggler.

But by the time the group crossed into Turkey, they were intercepted by Turkish border patrol. Payam ended up in a Turkish prison for several months, facing deportation back to Iran. If he returned, God knows what would have happened to him—interrogation, torture, the full weight of the system that had already decided he was disposable.

His family contacted the National Spiritual Assembly of the Bahá'ís of Turkey to intervene. They asked for letters, explanations, anything to prove this was a brilliant young man whose only "crime" was his faith. Lawyers were hired, even though they didn't speak Turkish. English was barely usable there. It was chaos and fear and helplessness all at once.

And then, a miracle. Instead of sending him back, the Turkish police handed Payam over to the UN office. He was granted temporary status. Months later, after interviews and waiting, he received asylum in the United States. Then news came that he was enrolled in CalTech, an institution with a reputation that carried all the way to the alleyway where I lived. Payam was a real-life shooting star.

My own desire to leave was hardening into certainty. The adults saw danger and loss in Payam's story, even with its happy ending. Their sons and daughters saw guts and hope. But with no license and no university to my name, I saw stars in my eyes of places like Berkeley or MIT. My thought experiment of escape was active in my mind. How fortunate was I to have an actual home country to return to? I was not a refugee; I was a citizen. *What am I waiting for?*

When I graduated from high school, it was anticlimactic. It was not a rite of passage but a feeling of being in quicksand. Not having enrolled in university nor being willing to join the military, I was not allowed to drive or get a job. This was because in order to be eligible for a driver's license, you either had to be registered as a student in a high school or university or registered for military service. My stagnation in Tehran without a driver's license was unbearable. I was grounded educationally and now physically, unable to move freely to work, to visit friends, to expand my mind in ways of my choosing.

With few options left, I returned to my high school to seek out Mr. Seifi, a strict yet fair administrator who had always respected my academic record—I had the second-highest GPA in the entire school and was first in my class.

I found him in his office, stacks of papers looming around him. "Mr. Seifi," I began, my voice tight, "I need your help. I want to go to university, but…I can't. As a Bahá'í, they won't let me in."

He raised an eyebrow, leaning back in his chair. "You… you're telling me they would just deny you because of your faith?" His voice was quiet, almost disbelieving. It surprised me how a man of his middle age having lived in Iran for all his life didn't grasp the discriminatory practices embedded in the system he was a part of.

"Yes," I said. "And I still need a driver's license," I added quickly, sensing the danger in asking. "I need to be able to get around, to keep living my life."

He rubbed his forehead, "If anyone finds out we are having this conversation…." He didn't finish the sentence, but I knew he could lose his position, face investigation, or even worse. I began to wonder if I was being too selfish.

I swallowed hard, my chest tight with regret. "I understand."

He studied me for a long moment, then his expression softened. "You graduated early, didn't you? Seventeen?"

"Yes." He was aware I had skipped a grade thanks to the kindness of Mr. Berenjian in second grade, who helped me find a new school after I was kicked out of the first.

He leaned forward, lowering his voice. "Come back tomorrow. Don't tell anyone. I'll see what I can do."

The next day, he handed me a plain envelope. "Here. It says you're still attending high school. Signed, stamped...my word."

I stared at him, realizing the enormity of what he'd just done. "Mr. Seifi...you're risking so much for me."

He gave me a tight, almost conspiratorial smile, then pulled me into a brief hug. "May the good Lord bless you."

Clutching that envelope like the passport it was, I walked into the motor vehicles office, every step weighed with anxiety. Would they know I was lying? They glanced at the document, their faces neutral, disinterested, and without another word, let me take the written test. Then the road test. And just like that, I emerged on the other side with my driver's license—proof that even under the watchful eye of an oppressive system, courage, and quiet workarounds could still carve a path forward.

A driver's license provided me with some semblance of normalcy. I used it to drive my sister to her music lessons and run errands, feeling freer than before.

* * *

Denied the traditional pathway toward higher learning, other Bahá'í youths and I turned to alternative means for seeking knowledge through underground study groups organized by the Bahá'í community and attending clandestine classes.

Where the Islamic Republic kept me out of higher education, the Bahá'í Institute for Higher Education (BIHE) provided hope and resistance in Iran. Not just an alternative educational institution, BIHE stood as a bold statement against systemic oppression experienced by Bahá'í communities across Iran.

Both my parents were among the first group of educated Bahá'ís who formed committees to found the BIHE in what seemed to be a logistical impossibility. However, they believed in the power of collaboration and in finding the potential within and outside of the Bahá'í community to develop curricula, course directories, registrar's documents, and an admissions process. BIHE became a university system that was unaccredited and unrecognized by the Islamic Republic, with no brick-and-mortar buildings anywhere to be found, run in the basements and homes of fellow Bahá'ís.

My involvement with BIHE marked an inflection point in my life. Here, I discovered an incredible community of learners and educators united by their mutual struggle for the pursuit of knowledge rather than a degree from an accredited university, in spite of persecution. Their classes were held clandestinely in homes or makeshift classrooms, which was a testament to the resilience and ingenuity of Bahá'í community members.

BIHE was more than an educational institution; it stood as a symbol of hope and defiance. We refused to be silenced; rather, we persevered despite any barriers put before us and learned despite any restrictions placed upon us. Volunteer educators risked their safety to teach because of a deep belief in the transformative powers of knowledge.

The passion and dedication of these educators, such as the president of BIHE, who, despite serving five years behind bars for his role in founding and running BIHE, continued teaching and inspiring. Unfortunately, his story wasn't the only one; many other BIHE educators and administrators also faced harassment, arrest, and imprisonment because of their commitment to providing Bahá'í youth an education.

My involvement with BIHE began when I volunteered to grade entrance exams, an essential process in upholding its integrity and academic standards. Exams would be distributed throughout Iran's Bahá'í communities, and local contacts administered them to groups of students at private homes before returning them for grading at central locations. Grading became something that gave me purpose while contributing to a larger fight for educational equality—something that gave me great pleasure as a teenager.

My mother played an essential role at BIHE. As a physician, she taught embryology and physiology to Bahá'í students. She would meticulously prepare lectures and instructional materials before using her office, which was on the ground floor of our home, as a makeshift classroom. There was a risk in bringing students together.

But she had finished her schooling decades before in the pre-Revolution era and needed to refresh herself on the material to be able to develop the course material. She bought the textbooks, revisited the material, and even took it upon herself to go to the office hours of some faculty in Iranian universities to gather materials. The faculty were inspired by her story and spirit of volunteerism, expressed regrets about systemic discrimination, and many of them provided assistance to her on the condition of anonymity. My mother used visual aids as part of her teaching methods, and that's where I came in.

To assist her, I created detailed paintings of embryological structures on large cardboard sheets; she would then use these paintings in her classes to help students visualize and understand complex concepts. I took pride in my work and even asked my mother to recognize me with credit for creating these masterpieces during her in-person sessions.

One time, the doorbell rang, and two bearded men in plain clothes emerged at the door while a BIHE class was underway. My father went over to them, and the men asked why young men and women were inside. Without missing a beat, he responded, "My wife is a university professor. The students sometimes arrange for question-and-answer sessions after hours in her office." The men promptly apologized and left. My father always said, "Place a firm foot in front of the most rabid animals, or they will devour you."

The regime was watching closely and found ways to intercept our rhythm, and our new system became a cat-and-mouse game of "catch me if you can." The post office was supposed to be a lifeline, a simple way for students to send their assignments and exams to BIHE professors across the country. But the post office became something the vultures would prey upon. Art projects, physics problems, and even essays that should have traveled safely vanished into thin air. Letters went missing. Packages never arrived. The mail had been intercepted.

At first, panic set in. How could our alternate university operate when its most basic functions—receiving homework and taking and grading tests—were under attack? Then, a workaround: a clandestine courier system.

Motorbikes were kick-started at dawn. Young men on two wheels became messengers in a covert war of knowledge. They weaved through Tehran streets, scaling stairwells, slipping through alleys, clutching envelopes and notebooks as if they were keys to the kingdom—and they were.

Sometimes a motorbike would vanish, stolen by the same vultures who patrolled the hiking trails, leaving its rider stranded and furious. Yet the couriers carried on, improvising, rerouting, finding new ways.

The irony was at BIHE, I was being taught and guided by brilliant minds—MIT graduates, renowned architects, engineers—people whose potential could have transformed a nation. And yet, in Iran, they were dismissed, barred from practicing their professions, and, as in the case of the BIHE president, imprisoned, simply for choosing to give back to their community.

Dr. Parviz Javid had a PhD in pharmaceutics from the University of Wisconsin. He had a small stature and poor eyesight. He had orthopedic limitations and walked with a characteristic gait. He, too, had joined the chorus of educators at the BIHE with care and resolve like a father figure. He would have been a national treasure to the entire nation had the Islamic Republic recognized his potential to contribute to the education of the next generation. When he became ill and was hospitalized in Tehran, hundreds of students lined up with flowers to visit him in his room. The hospital nurses and staff were puzzled and kept asking who the old man with so many young visitors was. When a community is under pressure from the outside, it sticks together. Much like when you raise the temperature and pressure on carbon, you can get diamonds. When there were members of the community on the run because they were being pursued, they would go to the homes of different members of the community unannounced and seek refuge.

When students of the Bahá'í institute would come to Tehran from the provinces to attend in-person classes, they would be housed by their spiritual aunts and uncles whom they had never met. Homes would be opened to students in need of housing and food. Our own home became host to many students over the years, and my sister and I would revel at their accents and sit and listen to tales of their journey and what it was like growing up in such places as Tabriz or Gonbad-e-Kavus.

From time to time, a young man from a province ten hours away appeared at our doorstep, dragging his feet across miles of road just to reach in-person BIHE classes. Dust clung to his shoes, and his backpack sagged with every step, but he never complained. We hardly even knew his name at first. He was just there, eager to learn. Eventually, the community found him a place to sleep, a small roof for his dedication to rest under, but even before that, his persistence spoke louder than words: Education was worth the journey, worth the hardship, worth everything. I knew, because I felt exactly the same way.

Nearing eighteen, on the cusp of official adulthood, the future felt suddenly close. I began to wonder how I could possibly build a grown-up life in Iran. I was already enrolled in the BIHE studying civil engineering, following in my father's footsteps, but what I really wanted was to follow in my mother's and the Berjises who came before her. Medicine had always pulled at me, but BIHE couldn't offer medical training, which meant my only option was outside Iran, back in America.

I knew my parents would never deny me the same education that so many of our relatives had pursued abroad. The time had come. All I needed now was the courage to tell them.

It was during this time of internal turmoil that I took regularly to the hiking paths to figure out my future. On one particular hike just past a rocky mountain stream, I listened to a bootleg of Iranian pop music from Persian musicians writing songs in exile out of Los Angeles. As I adjusted the volume, I didn't hear the vultures creep up behind me. Two agents tapped me on the shoulder and motioned for me to remove my headphones.

"We need to search your fanny pack," one agent said. As a religious minority, I was far more cautious than the average teen. Lacking the courage to refuse him, I removed the pack and let him investigate its contents. Finding nothing but chewing gum, packets of nuts, and lip balm, the agent pointed to my Walkman.

"What are you listening to?" the other officer asked, playing worse cop to his partner's bad cop. "Let us see the Walkman."

The agent pressed stop and eject and waved the cassette. "This is illegal music," he said, his tone that of my elementary headmaster about to tear up my transcripts. "You can't have this. Now it's ours."

With that, he took my cassette and my Walkman.

"Take the tape," I said, "but my Walkman is not illegal."

The agents looked at each other and then back at me as if I were a dangerous criminal, but the Walkman became so much bigger to me than just a device. It was the last straw.

"It is mine. Please return it to me," I said, my eyes steady, letting them see I wasn't going to back down.

"The Walkman will be in the trailhead office when you are done," the agent said. "Pick it up then."

I never saw those agents, nor my Walkman, again. It was the first time I became angry, impassioned with righteous indignation. If I had lived somewhere else, I could indulge in the simple pleasure of hiking without being frisked. I'd be permitted an Iranian passport so I could cross borders and never come back. I would be free to go to university to become a doctor like my mother, my grandfather, my great grandfather, and my great uncles.

And then my thought experiments became a plan.

* * *

As the hardness of my new sneakers stung my heels on the trek home, I hiked as if I were in training. A fire had lit inside me. I returned to the trail several times to focus on increasing my endurance, testing myself on muddier terrain and deeper inclines. The hiking and walking became less about meditation and thought and much more physical and purposeful, of someone who was going to cross over mountaintops. I logged my time and distance, manipulated my body temperature, allowing it to heat up and cool down, testing my discomfort all while minimizing my water intake. I once again found myself in a narrow valley, where I saw the vultures circle and land at my feet.

"Stop this instant," an agent said. "What do you have in your backpack?"

The agent placed both hands on my shoulders and spun me around so they could wrestle my backpack from me.

"What is this magazine?" the agent said, pulling out a tattered copy of *Rolling Stone.* "This is banned. Do you want us to arrest you? You know better than this."

Satisfied by my surrender of the contraband, the agents marched away. They thought they had fed on, as vultures do, the death of my spirits. Except they didn't know about the Berjis Big Red Spot—the unrelenting storm that lived in my chest.

When I got home from my hike, I pulled out a worn shoebox and held my American passport like a delicate gem. *This is my ticket out of here,* I thought. There was a reason that my parents had found workarounds to give me the freedom and opportunity to dream bigger, aim higher, and ultimately take charge of my destiny. There had been a reason my father insisted both his children were born with "choices." There had been a reason he kept my passport up-to-date through trips to the Swiss Embassy—the liaison to the American one in Bern, Switzerland. The reason was that my future was not here. It was time to stop looking at my passport—and start using it.

CHAPTER 7

"I need to leave Iran," I said to my father.

"You are chasing shadows, Nizam," my father said, his words weighted with fear. "Shadows that may swallow you whole."

"No, Baba," I said. "I'm looking for light, freedom, opportunity. Isn't that what we always desired?"

"You talk of freedom," he replied. "But once outside your safe home, you may only rely on yourself and your skills for survival."

"Baba, isn't that what freedom is?"

My father's eyes softened. "But, my son," he said. "You could be killed."

His words rose like a mushroom cloud, threatening to poison my hope. "Okay, Baba," I said, my throat on fire, "have it your way, then. But in the future, when you have a son who walks with his head down, drowning in depression with no career to call his own, no passion for work, days filled with regret, I will blame my failures on you. You will behold an empty adult, knowing I had once begged for fullness."

It was rare I ever spoke to my father so angrily and judgmentally, but being educated and trained was a timely issue for me. It is something you must do when you're young. If I waited until adulthood to leave, where would I wind up? And as what?

My unflinching father was scared, not of the Islamic Republic but of losing his only son. We were all scared from the story of Payam and the persecuted professors of the BIHE. We had heard stories of those who left with hearts full of hope and never made it across borders. We had heard of those who were shot, arrested, deported, and stripped of all livelihood. Either way, I felt doomed. If I didn't leave Iran, it would be the end of the ancestry of doctors in my family. If I were killed while being smuggled out of the country, it could be the end of the line of my father's last name. It would lead to a life of regret my father could never overcome. For the first time in my life, I spoke to my father, not as his son, but as a man to another man.

"Father," I continued, "in Iran, I am as good as dead."

"Then, my son, the decision is made."

The risk of death was worth the chance at life.

* * *

As soon as my family and I accepted the stakes of my escape, the question wasn't how to do it but who could help me. At home in our tight-knit community, where words spoken out loud could invite danger, the quest to leave Iran was shrouded in secrecy. We knew the Samavi family's two daughters had recently left Iran, so we met them in person to avoid discussing on phone lines that might be tapped by the government.

The Samavis suspected why we were there. Within our community, the desire for escape, to seek better lives elsewhere, was an understandable wish that didn't need further discussion. They shared their experience, telling us about the man who smuggled people out. "This guy was extremely professional; he took payment up front and delivered," Mr. Samavi told my father, as if he were giving a five-star restaurant review. "Our daughters arrived safely over there, and that's what matters."

"Over there" was Turkey, the border country to which many Iranians fled. If you were lucky enough not to be caught, like Payam, or killed, once in Turkey, the typical trajectory for refugees was to seek asylum at the United Nations office in Ankara. As a Bahá'í, I was not allowed an Iranian passport to easily travel into Ankara; and attempting to show my United States passport would not help me in departing from Iran. The Islamic Republic mandates that all people of Iranian descent have an Iranian passport to leave the country, and the Iranian passport was denied to those deemed nonhuman, like the Bahá'ís.

Relieved to have the honest word and referral of a fellow Bahá'í parent, my father asked Mr. Samavi, "Do you have his name and number?"

"Well, I don't know his name," answered Mr. Samavi. "He goes by Uncle Hadi, and I don't have his number either. But we've been a good referral source for him, so we expect he'll be calling soon. He was referred to us by another family in the same manner, and we will pay this favor forward. We will be sure to give him your number."

While we waited, my parents made a list of all the friends and relatives we knew who had fled Iran and settled in other parts of the world. Plan A was to utilize the smuggler the Samavis referred and have him transport me outside the country over the course of a few days and nights. In the best-case scenario, I'd be exhausted and alive. But we knew there were no guarantees of safety, so we needed plans in case my journey back to America was not a straight one. There was my uncle in Austria.

He would be a pitstop until I sorted out my American citizenship. There were trusted friends from the Bahá'í Institute who'd settled as far away as Los Angeles and Australia. And using codes in our letter writing, we mailed a letter to my mother's sister, also a pediatrician, who lived in Frederick, Maryland. I had only seen pictures of my aunt and cousins, but their home would become my home if all went as planned.

During these early planning stages of my escape, when my father reached in the depths of his closet to retrieve my American passport, he came across old black-and-white photos—dusty, fragile prints of the 1940s. He pointed to a baby in one frame, himself as an infant, propped on pillows. I asked, puzzled, "Who had a camera back then? Who is the baby on this chair? Did someone just happen to take those pictures?" He nodded slowly.

He told me something school curricula had deliberately omitted: There were Polish men in his childhood neighborhood, men who barely spoke Persian, carrying folders full of photos. They knocked on doors, introduced themselves, and offered to take family portraits—for just a few pennies or dollars. They were not professional photographers in the conventional sense; they were refugees, survivors, Jews who had found an unlikely haven in Iran. This is how my father, born in 1941, had a precious photo of himself as a toddler in his possession.

He explained that the presence of Polish Jews in Iran was linked to a remarkable man: Abdol Hossein Sardari, often called the "Iranian Schindler." Sardari was Iran's diplomat in Paris during World War II, and he played a critical, dangerous role in rescuing Jewish lives under Nazi occupation. Sardari did something nearly impossible. He used his diplomatic status to issue Iranian passports—many blank, many forged—not just to Iranian Jews, but to non-Iranian Jews as well. He argued absurdly—to Nazi officials—that Iranian Jews weren't "racially Jewish" in the way they understood it. He called them Djougouten: a made-up Aryan minority. And somehow, it worked. He saved somewhere between 2,000 and 3,000 Jewish lives.

My father paused. "That's how those men ended up in my neighborhood," he said quietly. "They had no plan to stay long, but they stayed enough to build lives, to marry locals, to take photos, and to be seen."

What struck me most was the irony. A man—an Iranian—had saved Jews by forging their identity, granting them safety and freedom in a time of genocide. And here I was, planning to smuggle myself out of Iran, compelled by persecution and lack of the same freedom Iran had historically afforded others. Once, this country had been an unlikely refuge for those fleeing horror; now, I was in a different era, and for me, it was a cage.

Sardari's courage was never taught to us Tulips of the Revolution in school. He didn't become a hero in our history books or a national icon, even though he risked everything. Instead, we were subjected to propaganda that taught hatred and denial, including toward the "religious minority" Jewish community in Iran, of which my own maternal family members were a part. My education, filled with slogans and maintained narratives, never made room for a story like Sardari's.

When I discovered this, it changed something in me. This wasn't just family lore; it was a historical and political fact. It was a powerful metaphor for what Uncle Hadi was doing: risking everything not just to help people escape but to reclaim freedom and, most importantly, hope.

Backup plans and worst-case scenarios plotted out, Uncle Hadi finally called. The only words spoken were of my father's invitation to visit our home. For days, Hadi had been this shadowy figure in my imagination, but when he arrived, I was surprised by how he reminded me of an approachable middle-aged neighbor, complete with an inviting smile that said, "I'm happy to see you; let's break bread."

Hadi, which in Persian means "guide," was a chameleon, changing his name and his appearance frequently to keep ahead of the vultures. With his curly hair and rosy cheeks, he did not look like someone who told secrets and lies, like some cartoon villain with a handlebar mustache smoking a cigar. He was risking his life breaking the law in order to help us break the law. But, instead of an outlaw, we regarded him as a Robin Hood, with virtuousness wrapped around his violations. Except, instead of stealing money from the rich and giving it to the poor, Uncle Hadi was dealing in the currency of freedom while he took the talented youth from oppressors and handed them to countries eager to gain from future doctors, engineers, and researchers.

Hadi, like so many, was well aware of the problem of "brain drain." He had sensed this business opportunity and made a lucrative life for himself, but not without daily risk. The fact that Hadi had as much to lose as we did helped my parents put my life in his hands. Hadi demanded all of the money in cash with no receipt up front. It was not easy talking my father into this arrangement.

"What if I give you this significant sum, and we never hear from you again?" my father asked, his voice meek.

Hadi replied, "That is the risk you take."

And now, with this strange man with no name, no identification, no contact information, asking for "cash up front," without knowing if he would ever call again, the unknowns made us question our sanity.

"We will do this by oral agreement," Hadi explained, as he laid out the terms in our living room. "I need passport-style photos of Nizam for documents that I will arrange. The Iranian passport I secure for him will be real, but it will only serve him as identification in Turkey. It cannot be used at the border to go through Iranian passport control. Once I make this passport and the conditions are right, I will connect with further instructions."

Hadi put his hand out to shake my father's hand. "Wait for my call," Hadi said as we showed him to the door. "And don't tell anyone, not even those closest to you."

For weeks, I was trapped inside a secret. Eating with my grandmother, knowing it could be the last time, without telling her my plan, was excruciating. When the phone rang and it wasn't Hadi, my mother sat to wipe her brow. Pretending with my friends like everything was normal, only to know I'd disappear one night, weighed on me. I withdrew so I wouldn't risk giving myself away. When we went for groceries with little money, we imagined Hadi had spent our fee on the best cheeses and meats money could buy. Time slipped away along with our hope in Hadi.

Then, when we were about to give up on ever seeing Hadi again, he called on an ordinary Wednesday afternoon. "Arrive at the bus station in Tabriz by noon this Friday."

* * *

I examined my bedroom, scanning its understated walls. Everything suddenly seemed significant—my twin-sized bed beneath my window, my overflowing closet, my secret poster of Madonna as The Material Girl, boasting her strings of diamonds and pearls and long satin gloves. My hands glided over old puzzles, my favorite toy race cars, and, hidden at the bottom of a box, an old copy of *Playboy* with its worn pages partially detached at the spine. *What if my parents found it after I am gone? Can I hide it in the trash before I go?* I worried that if I were killed, my poor grieving mother would stumble upon it when cleaning out my things. What would she think of me in death? I decided to take my chances and leave the magazine buried in a box within a box. Fate would handle it.

Suddenly, I was nostalgic for the nights when my mother's hand would reach for me under the bed, guiding me to the stairwell where she'd huddle with me on her lap. How often had I sat at my desk, poring over mathematics and drinking up poetry and literature? If I ever made it back to America, I could prove my worth and hopefully find a workaround for my lack of proper academic records. Even though I didn't have a degree, my parents had stayed focused on making sure I was educated. I might not have had a piece of paper saying I graduated high school or a transcript, but I was learned. My parents knew that knowledge itself is a passport. Now, I wanted to use it and prove I was capable of becoming a doctor.

There was only room for one small suitcase, so I could only pack items of minimal material value—clothes, an extra pair of shoes, underwear, socks, and essential toiletries. My mother cleverly sewed $800 into the waistband of my jeans, so if anyone reached into my pockets, they wouldn't find anything. Additionally, my US passport—my golden ticket to a new life—was concealed deep within layers of doubled underwear fabric, safe from a casual body pat down. If I concealed it safely, my passport would save me. If it were found, the same passport could be my trap.

It wasn't until I watched my mother painstakingly open the seams in my pants, creating hidden compartments to hide my money and passport, did the danger sink in. What had I gotten myself into? As she resewed the waistband with the precision of a surgeon, my mother caught me staring from the doorway. Attuned to the heaviness inside me, she gripped my jeans in her hands and said, "Tell me what is going on inside that head, Nizam."

"Maman, what if I don't make it?"

"You will make it, my son."

"What if I don't?"

"Nizam, we are together in this," she said, her quiet conviction carrying me back to the place inside my heart that felt like hope. She was the forward-thinking ying to my father's cautious yang.

One of the reasons my father never wanted me to leave Iran, especially as a minor, was simple: You could get caught. And getting caught didn't just ruin your own life; it could devastate the entire family. He'd say, "They could put you in jail. They could take our house. They might even make us put the house up as collateral for your release. And then you'd spend months, maybe years, trapped in the Revolutionary Courts. They could arrest your mother and me or both of us, leaving your sister all alone."

But my being eighteen took some of the weight off my parents. No longer legally responsible for me, it could be argued that leaving was my own decision, my own conspiracy against the regime, and if caught, my own crime to be hanged for. If I had done this when I was a minor, the liability was my family's burden and the price would be theirs to pay. My father saw what had happened to Payam and doubled down on his fear for me.

"If this happens to you," he said, "I could never live without my only son."

The plan was for donkeys to carry my bag over the mountains as I hiked in darkness for eight or more hours to cross from Iran into Turkey illegally. Once in Turkey, I'd use my fake Iranian passport secured by Uncle Hadi as a form of ID at checkpoints while making the bus journey to Ankara. Once in Ankara, I would return that fake passport to one of Hadi's ambassadors, then take myself with my American passport to the United States Embassy. I'd wear my jeans, a light jacket, and, of course, my off-brand sneakers. I had trained in them on the Alborz Mountain trails, my endurance as broken-in as the leather and soles.

During our last supper together in Tehran, my family passed the food around as we would any other Thursday evening. Our silence spoke what we couldn't in words: This could forever be our last meal together as a family. My sister and father silently cleaned their plates and left my mother and me alone in the dimly lit kitchen. She was reading my face, which wore the same forlorn expression I had when we left the principal's office in first grade and then again in middle school, and yet again in search of another replacement high school. Unprompted, my mother said, "Nizam, I see the same fire in you that propelled me to pursue medicine and dream beyond what life handed to me."

She knew of the risks inherent in taking on the journey back to America and of its costs in terms of lives left unfulfilled and unrealized. She had been the first person to lay eyes on me, and as I looked at her now, we both understood that even if I made it alive, this might be the last time.

"I will never stand in the way of your dreams," she said, her voice a whisper. "Your father and I have always wanted more for you and your sister than this place could provide. Now, I recognize that your spirit cannot be contained by walls of any fear that may seek to restrict us."

My parents were not only giving me permission to leave; they were delivering me to my destiny.

PART II

LOOKING AHEAD

CHAPTER 8

Uncle Hadi's men gestured for me to enter the back of a truck parked behind the bus terminal in Tabriz. My father and I hugged goodbye, like two familiar friends after a card game, casual, without fanfare, so as not to draw attention. As my father walked away, I watched his shadow grow long on the asphalt, then fade, committing its shape to memory in case this was the last time I would see him.

We climbed into the back of the truck and disappeared beneath a canvas tarp that dropped us into instant darkness. We were told to lie flat and pull it down low, to make ourselves indistinguishable from a load of dirt. Above us, the canvas did double duty—shield and blindfold, hiding us from prying eyes while erasing the world we were leaving behind.

The darkness pressed in, familiar in a way I hadn't expected. My body knew this posture before my mind did. Under the tarp felt like under the bed during the Iraq bombings—waiting, still, listening for what might come next. Back then, my mother would reach for me in the dark, her hand finding mine, steady and sure, a wordless promise that I was not alone. Now, flattened beneath canvas instead of furniture, I reached for that memory.

There was no hand this time—only the echo of it, lingering long enough to keep me still.

A Bahá'í friend of mine named Mojgan was the only familiar face. She was two years older than I and was also escaping to pursue higher education. We had grown up together, going to youth camps and gathering in each other's homes to play instruments and read poetry as our parents provided safe places to socialize with our peers and be ourselves without paranoia and fear. The other strangers sat side-by-side, united in their pursuit of freedom. Once my eyes adjusted, silhouettes of fellow travelers formed—fifteen in total, some families, and one single parent with a small child. The brakes released. The truck nudged forward. My mind drifted to my family.

I was pressed back into the corner of the truck, knees to my chest, trying not to shake. I could feel the cold metal of the Bahá'í pendant beneath my shirt, the one I'd worn for years but never dared to show. Instinctively, my fingers go to it—small, gold, smooth on one side and rough on the other. Touching it steadied me, and with that touch came another memory.

Before I ever dreamed of escaping Iran, I used to tutor algebra and physics. One of my students was a girl my age undergoing radiation and chemotherapy—blood cancer, maybe leukemia. Because her immune system was too fragile for school, her parents hired me to teach her at home. She always wore a mask; I always washed my hands twice before starting. She was lovely, gentle. I still hope she survived.

Her family paid me in cash, always tucked into a small envelope. But Iran's currency was collapsing—whatever I earned lost value by the day. So every few weeks, I would take the saved bills and buy a little gold. That's how I found Kamal, the jeweler.

His shop wasn't on the main street but tucked inside a narrow passage—a tiny, twisting arcade of shops you had to weave through. I'd walk down the dim corridor, past the smell of soldering metal and old carpet, until I reached his counter.

One day, I brought him a scrap of paper, an image I had found in an old Bahá'í magazine from before the Revolution. I had shrunk it on a Xerox machine until it was pendant-sized.

"I want this made," I said, laying it carefully on the counter.

Kamal picked it up, the metal scale in his hand stilled. He recognized it immediately—a Bahá'í ring symbol. Illegal. Dangerous. Contraband. He lowered his voice. "You know what this is," he said. "And you know what it means for me if anyone finds out I made it."

"I won't tell anyone," I said. "And I'm certainly not here to trap you."

Kamal studied me to determine whether I was an agent trying to test him. One wrong decision and his shop could be closed, his livelihood gone.

Finally, he nodded. "All right. Come back next week. Half now, half when it's done."

When I returned, Kamal placed the pendant in my hand. It was beautiful, but the edges were sharp enough to scratch skin.

"What are we going to do about this?" I asked.

"If I file the edges," he said, "you'll lose some of your gold. Why not make more money, and I'll build a small frame around it."

So I kept tutoring, kept saving, kept coming back. Each week he worked on it a little more—smoothing, framing, shaping—until finally it was finished: a small gold emblem of the faith of my family, made in secret. I hung it on a chain, which

I also earned enough money to purchase, always hidden under my shirt.

This ride was going to be rough. My pendant reminded me that roughness is not permanent; with work and determination, one can level mountains and fill valleys. From beneath the canvas, I spoke to the truckload of fellow passengers, nameless cohorts of freedom.

"Why don't we go around saying our names and where we are from?" I suggested. It was my own version of filing down the sharp tension that pierced the air and an icebreaker I had picked up from our youth group camps outside of Tehran. Mojgan instantly knew the game and went first. We exchanged names and hometowns, each voice and accent revealing varied origins from Tehran to Zanjan and Shiraz—a microcosm of Iran on the move.

The truck swerved violently, then ground to a halt. A flat tire. The fragile levity I'd tried to summon evaporated in an instant. We were no longer moving; no longer hiding. Sitting ducks. *Is this the moment everything unravels? Will we get caught now that we've stopped?* My back felt like a knife was being dragged along my nerves, the pain sharpening with every second I stayed folded inside the truck. Fear or not, I couldn't stay still. I climbed out to straighten my spine, aware of how exposed that made me. Nearby, an unmarked sedan—the smugglers' car—idled as the driver worked on the tire. I didn't know if they were there to protect us…or to abandon us. Inside the truck, someone lit up a cigarette.

With the tire finally repaired, we assumed our positions shoulder to shoulder, and the truck ventured onward. A knee was in my ear, the smoker's lighter pressed against my back. Time seemed to move slowly as it changed with each hour's passage from city streets into unknown and unpredictable landscapes beyond.

Within our small space, stories unfolded in whispers, each tale weaving its way into an intricate tapestry of desperation that had led us there. A young couple barely older than me shared tales of education banned under their regime and how love continued in defiance against its attempts at controlling them; a middle-aged man spoke out frantically against loss and persecution that left his voice shaking; the family from Shiraz spoke of needing to abruptly leave their hometown for Tehran as their home was set on fire by Islamist zealots provoked by the Imam at the neighborhood mosque. All except one of our fifteen co-escapees were Bahá'ís.

Our truck came to a rolling stop. The engine's lull was more frightening than its violent rumble. Through the canvas, we heard muffled voices at a checkpoint but could make out no discernible language. Tension rose as we lay motionless, waiting for the unknown before Mojgan spoke up with a whisper: "We'll make it through," she promised with hopeful confidence. "We must."

The first time I felt the sharp edge of the unknown was during one of our many trips to the Caspian Sea, those makeshift family caravans we preferred over organized tours. Two or three cars packed with relatives and close friends. Those drives north were their own kind of adventure, each mile marked by anticipation, the sense that freedom lived somewhere on the other side of the mountains.

I was seven. It was 1983. The adults unfolded blankets and settled into their conversations, while I hovered at the shoreline, letting the waves chase my ankles. The Caspian felt like an endless playground, one that promised delight so long as you didn't wander too far.

Of course, I wandered too far.

The drop-off was sudden. One second, the water hugged my knees; the next, it tugged at my hips, then my stomach. The undertow found me. In a blink, I was slipping outward, my toes clawing at nothing. Panic clamped down on my chest. I wasn't thinking of my short life or anything poetic like that; what filled me instead was a cold, rising terror of what might be beneath me, beneath the surface I could no longer keep my head above. A fear of everything I didn't know, couldn't see, couldn't fight.

I tried to shout, but the sea swallowed the sound. My arms thrashed for something solid—an arm, a float, the shore—but the water kept pulling like a bully I couldn't beat. The sky was the water, the water the sky, as I tumbled and lost the way up.

And then I saw Shirin—our family friend and mother figure. She was sprinting toward the water. Even wrapped in the heavy, mandated layers of the Islamic Republic—robe hanging, headscarf clinging—she didn't hesitate. She plunged in fully clothed, pushing through the weight of her fabric with a force I had never known she possessed. I remember the shock of seeing her move like that, her determination slicing through the waves while I floundered helplessly.

Her arm reached me just as my legs gave out. Her grip was firm. Together we fought our way back to the shore, the sand under our feet, free from the threat of death. She brushed the wet hair from my eyes and asked quietly, "Are you okay?"

I nodded, though I wasn't sure yet. My body was safe, but the water had shown me, for the first time, how quickly the known could drop away into a void. And now, all these years later, locked inside the darkness of this truck, I felt that same undertow rise inside me—the same pull into the unknown, the same terror that this time the sand of freedom won't be beneath my feet.

The truck's brake released. Gravel crunched again beneath the tires. The memory released its grip as the present pressed back in. As we picked up some speed, the air slipped through the seams of the tarp and bit us with its icy tooth. We had driven deeper into the mountain range, where the thin elevation left us cold and dizzy. As evening approached, our journey took us to a secluded hut near the border. There, a family speaking neither Persian nor any language we understood welcomed us with a warmth that transcended words; their home became our brief respite during an otherwise uncertain journey. They prepared dinner for us. However, due to fear of food poisoning or illness, Mojgan and I decided to eat some nuts and raisins that we had brought with us. We received a briefing on what lay ahead, specifically that our carry-on-size suitcases would be loaded onto mules or donkeys, and we would leave on foot at 8:00 p.m.

Mojgan insisted they were horses, yet due to the dim light and tension of the moment, I didn't care to argue. These animals, whether mules or not, carried our few belongings and the women, including Mojgan. She appeared off-center as she perched awkwardly atop one of the mules. The path turned upward, leading us through sparse landscapes into barren mountains that stared down upon us, indifferent to our struggle.

This hike would be very different than the ones in the valley with my friends. There would be no yodeling, no catching our echoes. But one thing I was sure of: There would likely be vultures lurking.

Led by our nameless guide, my fellow escapees and I waited for darkness to fall before we set out to climb the mountain.

Even my young, trained legs throbbed and burned after eight hours of hiking untamed terrain, guided only by night vision and the donkeys carrying our modest belongings. I could sense the strain of the woman in front of me, who carried her two-year-old on her hip, the weight of her baby's future hers to carry. The couple in their fifties behind me took labored inhales as they were forced to keep up with the group or else be left behind. On the other side of the mountain was the nation of Turkey, where our guide would seek out the border guards who had been bribed to look the other way. If we were caught, the Turkish government would deport us to Iran, where we could face imprisonment or death.

Each step we took behind the mules felt like moving a chess piece in a high-stakes game in which the prize was freedom. But at what cost? My suitcase bobbed within a large burlap sack straddled over the animal's back. My belongings were of minimal material value—clothes, an extra pair of shoes, underwear, socks, and toiletries. I did not want the weight of books to slow me down, so my library remained home. I hoped my sister would enjoy some of the classics I had collected and think of me.

Before us stood a majestic mountain, its slopes shrouded in darkness against the starlit night. The air was cool, an unexpected contrast to the city where we had come from; each breath felt liberating as I inhaled the thin night air. The smog over Tehran obscured most stars and delivered disappointment when Halley crossed our skies. But the skies hovering over us in the elevation of Azerbaijan mountains were magnificently starlit as if millions of glass particles lit up the night sky and constellations came to life.

Our journey began with an excruciating climb through dark landscapes in single file as we had been advised, tracing the footsteps of silhouettes before us. My no-name sneakers had trekked similar terrain, but I had not trained in the pitch of night. Every step was carefully considered, mindful of loose stones or uneven ground that threatened to expose our presence at any misstep. I navigated my body using proprioception. My muscles burned from the uphill climb, each step taking us further from familiar memories and closer to an unknown future.

Silence reigned, broken only by our labored breathing and the occasional crunch of boots on the rocks. Communication took place primarily through gestures, nods, and hand signals, which sufficed to relay messages of encouragement or caution.

As we climbed higher, the terrain became increasingly challenging and fatigue set in; the path narrowed until there was barely enough room for single-file walking. I thought about how naïvely I had hiked with my friends, thinking I was training muscle memory. If it weren't for our guides' familiarity with the route, I would have gotten lost in the wilderness, left to die. I worked hard to banish these intrusive thoughts as memories of escapees abandoned mid trek would race through my mind.

We hiked for seven to eight hours through the night, guided only by our night vision, mules, and three of Uncle Hadi's men. My attempt at checking the time backfired when the faint glow from my digital watch caught one of our guides' eye. He stopped and looked like he wanted to rush me. He sliced his hand across his neck, as if to say we would die because of my slip-up. He whispered that the slightest light could look like a torch from afar and expose the entire group to the scrutiny of men with binoculars. Although he let me keep my watch, I learned my lesson.

As we drew nearer to the summit, our guides' fingers pressed against their lips...*shhhh*. An armed border guard stood motionless against the mountains. I could feel his eyes on us, permitting our passing but with obvious disdain.

Our passage had been paid for with bribes, adding to the tension at that moment, serving as a stark reminder of all the risks and how fragile the line between success and capture could be. Once we reached the summit, the large burlap sacks containing our carry-on luggage were unloaded from the mules and transferred to the helpers. The mules went back with one of Hadi's men, and the women joined the men to continue the trek on foot. At one point when we had passed the summit and started to descend, one guide turned to us, his hand becoming a human stop sign. "Sit quietly," he whispered. His eyes darted in the direction of unexpected men. He motioned toward the only cover in sight: a line of knee-high scrub clinging to the slope. We flattened ourselves behind it, dust puffing up as stone bit into our palms, pretending this thin disguise could make us invisible.

These were not the border guards Hadi knew. The vultures were back. Unlike my previous run-ins, these agents were not interested in confiscating my Walkman or harassing my friend for singing in the valley. They were not interested in exuding power for power's sake. This time, they were hunting. Hunting for dissidents considered traitors to Iran; hunting for infidels, for the unclean and inhuman Bahá'ís and Jews and Christians; hunting for women who dared to have agency over their bodies; hunting for American citizens, like me, whose passport to freedom threatened their way of life.

We all huddled together and trembled from a combination of dropping temperatures in the mountains and sheer terror. After about forty-five minutes, one of the guides motioned for us to resume our journey. Fatigue set in, making each step an effort. Together, we rallied, offering each other whispers of support and helping hands when necessary. When I ran out of water in the flask that was strapped over my shoulder, I asked the gentleman walking in front of me for some water. He poured some water from his flask into mine. When I quickly tried to gulp the water, my entire mouth burned. He was carrying hot water for his tea.

Leaving the country had been a monumental dream; however, crossing into Turkey was marked by an invisible line—nothing to note, see, or commemorate. It was ironic to me that a moment that marked a drastic change in the trajectory of my life had no physical marking at all.

I bent down and grasped a fistful of dirt so that I could feel, for the last time, the country that I loved unrequitedly. I stepped forward and just like that, the sands of freedom were beneath me. At least that's what I thought.

CHAPTER 9

Dawn broke and its first light cast its soft hue over the rugged terrain. Our group headed toward a small Turkish village, a collection of stone and mud houses and dirt paths offering shelter from what had been an excruciating night. As we approached, the barking of dogs from each property was audible in the eerie silence of dawn. Our guides led us toward a small earthen hut. Cramped and exhausted, we filed into its small space, barely finding room to rest from the fatigue of an exhausting night's trek.

Sitting directly on the ground, with no furniture to speak of, we leaned against the walls, trying to find some restful moments of relief from the elements outside. By dawn's light, our eyelids became heavy as adrenaline gave way to fatigue and exhaustion set in.

At 9:00 a.m., Hadi, the architect of our escape, reappeared as a messenger of hope, signaling that the most treacherous part of our journey had come to an end. He brought with him our passports: fake Iranian ones carrying our photos but with false names and dates of birth. "These passports all have fresh stamps from Turkey and will serve as your identification," Hadi informed us, an indication of all his careful planning to ensure our safe passage.

I knew that if I attempted to cross an international border using these fake passports, they would quickly be noticed as fraudulent; yet, in Turkey, they served their purpose well enough as identity documents that helped us blend in on the surface level.

Mojgan and I were listed as husband and wife on a single passport—a common practice for Iranian couples at the time and one that passed without question at borders. The irony wasn't lost on me. My own parents' marriage had never been officially recognized by the Islamic Republic because they were Bahá'í. On paper, their union didn't exist. And yet here I was, temporarily assigned a state-sanctioned intimacy with a stranger simply because it suited the system.

Hadi's method of recycling these passports was both ingenious and necessary for his revolving door of escapees. In a world where legitimacy was arbitrary and paperwork carried more weight than truth, survival depended on learning how to borrow the state's language—just long enough to pass through it.

As we sat in the hut, clutching our borrowed identities, the harsh reality of our situation dawned. We had traversed mountains, avoided border patrols, and placed our lives in the hands of strangers all to secure a safer future, and yet here we were, resting briefly before continuing our journey ahead. This humble shelter served only as a temporary refuge—one more step on a long and hazardous road ahead.

As we prepared to leave our hut with fake passports in hand, the complexity of our situation became evident. No longer were we fleeing persecution alone; now, we were illegal immigrants in a new land as part of a larger narrative and collective endeavor for freedom that transcended borders and identities. Our journey had changed us, bonding us together in search of an open future without fear.

A minibus arrived, taking us from this small, nearly forgotten village to Doğubeyazit; not just another dot on the map but a town bustling with a vibrancy close to Iran. By 10:00 a.m., it felt as if the day had truly begun. Our driver first took us to a telecommunications center, a place for people like us who had become displaced or separated from family. "Go and call your family," he instructed with an unspoken understanding that making those calls could bring much-needed relief.

By the time we entered the center, it had already reached noon. I imagined my family gathered around the phone, although without expectations since I had not promised a call this soon; yet here we were, about to break that silence much sooner than anticipated. Dialing my childhood home's number seemed like forever; finally, when it rang, I heard my father's familiar voice, and I said, "Baba, it's me."

He responded with disbelief and sheer delight: "Oh my God, my heart is racing out of my chest. Are you really there?" His doubtful tone betrayed a fatherly instinct of protection: "Are you just telling me this to make me feel better, or are you truly there in Turkey?"

As his concern tugged at my heart, I couldn't help but smile. "No, Baba," I assured him to ease his mind, hoping to assuage any fears about me being safe there. As proof, I mentioned something seemingly mundane yet profound—the sight of women walking freely without wearing the head coverings that Iran mandates. To most others, it may have seemed irrelevant. To us, it symbolized freedom from restrictions we had experienced back home.

Our conversation was brief but filled with emotion, providing a bridge to the distance between us. I told my dad that we would next go to Ankara aboard a much nicer bus than the one that took us to Doğubeyazit.

As we prepared for our next leg of travel while pretending to be husband and wife to avoid drawing unnecessary attention, I thought back on our checkpoint stops. Each time, the police would board our bus asking for our passports, sending chills down my spine every time. My heart would beat faster, yet our disguise remained intact, with all stamps passing the brief inspections without issue.

* * *

Ankara was like a bucket of ice water, shocking an arrested heart into a beat it didn't know it had. For the first time in my life, I was surrounded by people who were not afraid to be seen. Turkey in the early 1990s felt loud in a way Tehran never allowed itself to be—not just with sound, but with permission. The streets were layered with motion: buses coughing exhaust, vendors calling out in Turkish I couldn't yet decipher, snippets of German, English, Arabic, and languages I didn't recognize floating past me like radio stations I'd never been allowed to tune into. People walked with their shoulders loose, their bodies unguarded. No one seemed to be measuring every step.

The first thing I noticed was clothing. Women wore jeans and short skirts, loose blouses or tight tops, hair uncovered and styled with intention rather than compliance. Some wore lipstick so red it felt almost aggressive to my eyes, like the stains of pomegranate that didn't want to be washed out.

Men and women moved through the streets laughing loudly, arms linked, cigarette smoke curling from their fingers. Men dressed casually too—leather jackets, sneakers, unbuttoned shirts—no one trying to look pious, no one scanning the crowd for approval.

The air smelled different. Coffee, tobacco, grilled meat, diesel, perfume. Music spilled into the streets. From cafés and open windows came pop songs and rock riffs, Turkish ballads and Western beats, the bass bleeding into the sidewalk. At night, cafés stayed open late. People sat shoulder to shoulder at outdoor tables, drinking, arguing, flirting.

What struck me most wasn't the noise or the color, but how unpoliced the bodies were. No one corrected a sleeve, a strand of hair, the angle of a scarf. Women occupied space with their whole bodies—hips swinging, heads thrown back in laughter, hair catching the light. Men looked, yes—but looking was not a crime scene. Desire was not treated like a weapon. And that's when I realized how deeply trained my eyes were.

In Iran, I had learned early that the regime's agents did not always arrive in vans. As a child, I imagined danger as male—broad-shouldered silhouettes, unmarked cars, boots on gravel. But the Islamic Republic had its female vultures, too, draped in black from crown to heel, faces reduced to watchful eyes and a pale strip of nose. They moved through the streets with the same predatory calm, obeying the same instinct: to circle, to intimidate, to strike where fear was most fertile. The memory rose without warning.

I was in third grade the first time I saw them up close—not as an abstract threat but as hands reaching for my mother's dignity. She had come to pick me up from school, as she did every day after I had been quietly exiled from my first school and sent across districts. I remember the heat lifting off the pavement, her fingers wrapped around mine, the relief of being done for the day. Then the black silhouettes appeared.

"Sister—your hijab. Mind your hijab."

My mother kept walking.

They followed.

"Sister! Pull your scarf forward."

She stopped. Turned. "I am not your sister."

"We call you sister out of respect, sister!"

My mother, ever defiant, said, "Respect is when you honor my choice of clothing."

They warned her. Threatened custody. I remember how calmly my mother challenged with a question, "What exactly happens if a little of my hair shows?" They explained—without blinking—that her hair *stimulated men*, that this stimulation caused *problems*, that it was therefore *law*.

Mom replied, "Then your men have an illness. Perhaps the hijab belongs on their eyelids, not on my head."

In the end, she complied. Not because she believed them, but because survival required it. We walked to the car in silence. She started the engine. And then I asked the question no third grader should ever have to ask.

"Maman, what does it mean that men get stimulated?"

She didn't answer right away. When she did, her anger was precise.

"It means," she said, "that their sickness forces us to have conversations with our children long before we ever should."

Standing in Turkey years later, watching women move freely through the streets, many with their hair uncovered and some with hijab, that memory rearranged itself inside me. I understood something I hadn't fully grasped then: The vultures weren't just there to enforce dress codes. They were there to steal childhood. To seed fear early. To make the body shameful and controlled.

Here, the body was just a body. Nothing proved that more than the tourists, especially the American ones. Americans stood out immediately—not because of volume, but because of ease. Shorts. Baseball caps. Sneakers as a national identity. They walked as if the world owed them nothing. They spoke without lowering their voices, argued with maps, laughed at the wrong moments. They didn't look over their shoulders. They didn't calculate exits, even in a land that was not their own. They didn't flinch. I watched them the way you watch an illusion waiting to be revealed.

Was this what it meant to belong somewhere? I wondered if, in a matter of days, I would look like them—not in dress or accent, but in posture. If my shoulders would eventually forget how to brace for a tap.

I was eighteen and overwhelmed, not celebratory. Turkey wasn't a party town to me; it was a training ground. I was still coming off the mountain, still sleeping lightly, still counting money, still measuring time by uncertainty. But everywhere I turned, the world was insisting on coloring my imagination.

The Taç Hotel offered a temporary pause—four walls, thin curtains, and a bed that felt almost luxurious after days of movement. Hadi had paid for two nights, just enough time to breathe, just enough time to realize that whatever safety we had found was already expiring. By morning, it was clear our paths were about to split.

As planned, Hadi arranged for everyone in our group to report to the United Nations office, the usual next step for people like us—people without countries, without papers, without certainty. I packed quietly, aware that my destination was different.

"Why not the UN?" the smuggler asked, genuinely confused.

"I'm an American citizen," I said. "I have a passport."

He stared at me, trying to reconcile the sentence with the boy standing in front of him—mud still on my shoes, exhaustion etched into my face. Then he shook his head slowly, as if I'd just told him I was walking out of a war zone through a hidden door he'd never noticed. "You should have told me. I could have gotten your American passport stamped."

Still, trust was a luxury none of us could afford. Too much depended on things going right. Hadi, operating from a distance like a quiet conductor, had already played his part—making sure our documents carried the right stamps, the right impressions, the right lies and truths to pass inspection if anyone looked too closely. Paper, ink, timing. Survival reduced to details. While the others left for the UN office, I set out alone toward the American embassy.

The closer I got, the heavier the air felt—thick with urgency, with hope sharpened into desperation. From a distance, I could already see the line. It stretched down the block and around the corner: men clutching folders, women holding children by the shoulders, families standing shoulder to shoulder as if proximity itself could improve their chances. Faces from every corner of Iran. Eyes trained forward. No one wasted breath on conversation.

Every morning, scores of Iranians lined up outside the US embassy in Ankara just to take a number, just to ask for the possibility of an appointment. Since the revolution—since the embassy raid and its closure—this was the pilgrimage route. Hope now required travel.

Instinctively, I took my place at the end of the line, my American passport folded carefully in my hand, as if it might vanish if I looked at it too directly. I stood there absorbing the weight of it all—the silence, the waiting, the shared hunger for a door to open.

Then the man beside me glanced down. His eyes caught the navy-blue cover. He froze.

"That's an American passport," he said quietly.

I nodded.

He looked at me for a moment longer, then gestured toward the front of the line. "You don't belong back here," he said. "You can go straight in."

For the first time in my life, a government building did not repel me. It did not threaten me. It did not demand proof of loyalty or humiliation as an entry fee.

I stepped out of the line and walked forward, past the faces still waiting, past the silence thick with want. I didn't feel triumphant. I felt the weight of what I had been given without having earned it and the responsibility it carried.

Inside, past security, past the metal detectors and clipped instructions, I would soon meet a woman named Lucy. She would be the first official to look at me not as a problem to be managed, but as someone who already belonged.

Instead of directing me to one of the glass cubicles where voices were flattened by glass partitions and bureaucracy, Lucy led me down a short hallway and into her office. She closed the door behind us, sat, and motioned for me to do the same.

"Tell me again," she said, folding her hands on the desk, her voice calm but precise. "How did you get here?"

I took a breath. My English fractured under the weight of the story, but I began anyway—Iran, the mountains, the truck, the border, the waiting. I watched her eyes as I spoke, trying to read what each detail cost me.

She stopped me gently. "Slow down," she said. "You're safe here."

I nodded and continued, filling in what I could, skipping what I didn't yet have language for. When I finished, she picked up my passport and turned it over in her hands—not inspecting it, exactly, but acknowledging it.

"You understand," she said carefully, "that leaving Iran the way you did is one thing." She looked up at me. "But entering Turkey without authorization is another."

"I know," I said quickly. "I didn't have a choice."

"I believe you," she replied. Then, softer: "but Washington still has to be consulted."

She glanced at the clock on the wall. "It's too early there right now. I can't make any decisions until I speak with them."

My stomach tightened.

"Come back tomorrow morning," she said. "We'll talk again."

I wanted to ask her what that meant—for my future, for my freedom—but she was already standing, already signaling the end of the meeting. Before opening the door, she paused.

"We'll find a way," she said. Not a promise. But not nothing either.

Outside the embassy, I found a phone and called home. My father listened without interrupting as I told him everything—Lucy, Washington, the waiting.

Then he said, quietly, "What if the passport you're holding… disappears?"

I didn't answer.

"If you report it lost," he continued, "they issue a new one. Clean. No questions about how you entered Turkey or why your passport is missing a stamp. Surrender the old passport to the embassy and exit Turkey with the new one."

I returned to the embassy the next morning and told Lucy what my father had suggested.

She leaned back in her chair, considering it. "That's…ingenious," she said finally. Then she met my eyes. "But it only works if you're willing to follow through."

"I am," I said.

She nodded once. "Go to the central police station. File a report for a lost passport. Bring me the paperwork. Also, I will need a passport photo. Get that done too."

As I stood to leave, she added, almost as an afterthought, "This embassy is your sanctuary for now. Don't forget that."

I didn't.

* * *

The taxi ride to the police station passed in fragments—street signs I couldn't read, voices on the radio I didn't understand, the dull thump of my heart keeping time in my chest. My American passport was pressed flat against my skin, hidden deep inside my clothes, its presence both reassuring and terrifying. I was about to walk into a police station and report it lost.

The building smelled faintly of dust and disinfectant. Fluorescent lights hummed overhead. I was led to a small desk and motioned into a chair across from a female police officer. She looked tired, efficient. Her English, I quickly realized, was limited.

Good, I thought. *Very good.*

She asked me to state my name. I did. Then she asked why I was there.

"I lost my passport," I said, carefully, keeping my voice steady. "Near the Taç Hotel."

She nodded and started typing. Each keystroke echoed. My hands shook—not from this lie, but from a previous one—my body replaying the day I'd stood at the motor vehicles office with forged transcripts, learning how fear lodges itself in muscle memory. "Date of entry into Turkey?" she asked without looking up.

The question landed like a trapdoor opening beneath me.

To anyone else, it was routine. To me, it was perilous.

I knew the year—it was 1994. That much I was sure of. But months and days in the Gregorian calendar had never anchored my life the way they did here. My sense of time was shaped by a different rhythm, a different system. The Iranian calendar had differently named months, and they didn't coincide with Gregorian ones. If I were an American in Ankara with a lost passport, how could I not know the date the rest of the world readily knew? My cover could be blown in an instant. I hesitated.

She glanced up.

"When did you arrive?" she repeated.

"I…arrived the Saturday before last," I said, buying time. My eyes dropped to my hands as I counted silently on my fingers, trying to reconstruct my own movements.

She reached for a paper calendar beside her and began flipping pages.

"This Saturday?" she asked.

"No," I said quickly. "Before that."

She flipped again, then stopped. "August thirteenth?"

My breath caught. "Yes," I said, a fraction too fast, but she didn't seem to notice.

She typed again.

"How did you enter Turkey?"

"By airplane."

"What airline?"

My mind went blank.

I had never flown internationally before. I didn't know the names of airlines the way other people did. This was a world I had never been allowed to enter—until now.

I lifted my chin and took a gamble. "Turkish," I said.

She paused. Just for a second. Then she nodded and continued typing with her gaze fixed on the black and green monitor.

The room felt warmer. Or maybe that was just my blood rushing back into places it had abandoned.

She printed a report, stamped it, and slid the paper across the desk toward me.

"I'm sorry about your passport," she said, almost kindly.

"Thank you," I replied, my voice barely audible while pondering how the policewoman's poor English helped significantly, as she didn't notice that my English wasn't fluent either.

I folded the paper carefully and held it against my chest as if it were fragile, or sacred, or both. Then I stood, walked out of the station, and didn't allow myself to breathe fully until I was back on the street—back in the chaos of Ankara, still free, still unexposed, still holding the thinnest thread between myself and the life I was trying to reach.

The police report bought me time, but time was not the same as safety. When I returned to the Taç Hotel, I approached the front desk knowing I would have to do something I hadn't planned for: ask to stay longer.

The clerk looked up at me expectantly.

"One more night," I said. Then, after a beat, "Maybe two."

He tapped at the register, did the math, and told me the price. It was more than I wanted to spend, but less than the cost of being careless. I nodded and handed over the money, watching it disappear with the faint dread that came from knowing every folded bill retrieved from the inseam of my pants mattered now.

Upstairs, the hallway smelled of cigarette smoke and detergent. Mojgan was already in the room when I opened the door.

We looked at each other for a moment—two young people suspended between countries, rules, and futures—both of us exhausted, neither quite sure how to speak about what this moment meant.

"So," she said finally, forcing a small smile. "We're neighbors."

I let out a quiet laugh. "Apparently."

There was nothing improper about it. We were like siblings who happened to be playing house with a fake Iranian passport. As much as we tried to joke and laugh about the absurdity of it all, years of conditioning don't vanish just because you cross a border. In Iran, a boy and a girl sharing a room—even accidentally—was a crime waiting to be discovered. The fear followed us like a shadow, even here. And the grumblings of our fellow co-escapees snapped back into the habits of shaming and laws of tradition and modesty. "We haven't been here but hours and you are already acting Western," they'd say.

Mojgan set boundaries without naming them. She took one side of the room; I took the other. Shoes lined up carefully. Bags zipped and unzipped quietly. We spoke in lowered voices, as if the walls still had ears.

"What did they say?" she asked.

"At the police station?"

"Yes."

I pulled the folded paper from my pocket and showed it to her. She didn't touch it, just looked.

"So now what?"

"Now," I said, sitting on the edge of the bed, "I wait until morning. And hope Washington wakes up in a good mood."

She nodded, then sat, too, hugging her knees. "At least you have a passport. My visit to the UN office was long and painstaking. They've given me a temporary paper, and God knows when I will get called for an interview, if I will get accepted, and where I would get placed as a refugee."

I didn't answer right away. I nodded in sympathy.

I thought of the shoebox. Of my father's insistence. Of all the reasons that had led me here.

"Yes," I finally said. "But still, it feels like my passport could disappear just as easily."

The room grew quiet again. Outside, Ankara moved on—cars passing, voices drifting up from the street, music leaking from somewhere far below. A city alive with possibility, indifferent to our fear.

We lay down fully clothed, lights off, backs turned politely away from each other. Sleep came in fragments. Every sound made me alert, as if I were waiting for red sirens to sound off. Morning would decide everything. Until then, the Taç Hotel—cheap walls, shared air, borrowed time—was all I had.

CHAPTER 10

I walked back into the embassy clutching the police report like a talisman. In my naïveté, I believed this was the final step—that paper of lies, stamped and official, would simply unlock the rest of my life.

Lucy read it carefully, her brow tightening just slightly. "This will work," she said at last. Then she paused. "But not today."

I felt my chest tighten.

"A replacement passport takes four to five business days."

Four to five days. The words landed like a blow. I nodded, pretending I understood. I was doing the math in my head. August already half gone, university enrollment windows were closing, school calendars were ticking forward without me. Time was not a neutral thing anymore. It was my enemy. I had lied to survive, and the lie was now demanding I have patience.

Lying had always unsettled me. It was the currency of the Islamic Republic—lies layered over hypocrisy, rules enforced only on the powerless, virtue demanded publicly and discarded privately. I had grown up watching it. We all had.

Years later, when leaked footage surfaced of Ali Shamkhani's daughter's wedding—her plunging neckline on display, her mother's hair uncovered—the duplicity was undeniable. The very people who policed morality as the closest allies of the Supreme Leader lived above it. And now here I was, playing the same game. But my duplicity had different names: Survival. Escape. Education.

Lucy looked at me with a steadiness that felt almost maternal. "Come back tomorrow," she said. "We'll start the clock." I didn't understand English enough to know the metaphor, but she sounded a bit like a cowboy from the Spaghetti Westerns we watched through Mr. Zohrenejad's coaxial splitter. I stepped back into the August heat feeling hollow with all my hope wrangled in Lucy's lasso.

The days that followed stretched endlessly. I extended my stay at the Taç Hotel, counting bills carefully, calculating how long I could survive on bread and Coca-Cola. It was a terrible diet, but it was cheap and predictable. Every meal was a reminder: Make it last. Some afternoons, I found myself with other Bahá'ís—those waiting for the UN process to inch forward. Four-bedroom apartments were packed with ten people. One bathroom. The air was heavy with sweat and uncertainty. Refugee life.

One of the Samavi sisters was in one home I visited—the same sister who had escaped months before me and whose father's quiet referral had given my own father the trust to speak with Uncle Hadi. She served me boiled chicken with salt and pepper—the first real food I'd had in days. It was the best thing I had ever tasted. She was still waiting herself, bound for anywhere that would take her—the US, Australia, England—and in her patience I understood that a few more days of waiting was nothing. I was lucky. I knew that. I had a passport. I had a hotel, however cheap. I wasn't waiting months for an interview that might never come and the uncertainty of the file being approved. Still, the waiting gnawed at me.

At night, I replayed my father's words in my head when I first began to express that I wanted to leave Iran to answer my call to be a physician. "So many leave Iran to become doctors," he had said. "Some drive taxis. Some work in Persian restaurants in LA. The statistics are against you becoming a doctor. What makes you different?"

At the time, it felt like he doubted me. Later, I understood it for what it was: a challenge.

I loved my father dearly, respected his word, but in this case, I knew he was wrong, and I planned to prove it to him. I didn't realize he wanted to be wrong as well. Two days later, Lucy called my hotel, and I returned to the consulate. "You can go home now," she said, as she handed me my replacement passport. It was uncreased and stiff and smelled like hot glue. I now had two passports in hand. One, which my parents had secured on my behalf, with pages my father's fingertips had touched, his hope for our future as up-to-date as his love. And the second one, secured by me, thanks to a lie wrapped in a teenage dream. I surrendered the old passport to Lucy after I held it against my chest and thanked her for facilitating my exit. She smiled and embraced me, an act that was completely unfamiliar to me in any government building encounter in my life to that day.

My final step during my stay involved arriving in Istanbul and reaching out to my best friend Babak's uncle Fereidoun. With all the hotel and taxi expenses, I was short of cash, and Babak gave me his uncle's number in case I got into a jam. Uncle Fereidoun loaned me around $400 (which my parents repaid). He introduced me to the McDonald's Big Mac. The burger looked fake. Too round. Too shiny. Too large to be natural. Like it had been assembled by science, not a kitchen. Back home, bread had weight. It was sustenance. It was meant to be torn, to fight back. This bun just...surrendered, happy to be a garnish instead of the meal. The smell confused me. No garlic, no onions, no spices announcing themselves like they meant business. I took a bite. It tasted soft, sweet, and instantly comforting, like food that was designed with dopamine in mind. Compared to the food I grew up with—meals that took hours and demanded respect—this burger felt like cheating. How did they even ship this stuff? How do they make it taste the same everywhere? I didn't know whether to be impressed or offended. I just knew I wanted another one.

The challenge was booking an outbound flight on short notice. I didn't have enough money to afford upwards of $1,000 just for a plane ticket to the US. So, I called my father to figure out what to do. As usual, his advice was crafty.

"Head for Austria, where your Uncle Ezzat lives," he said. "We can plan the next steps from there." The price of a ticket to Austria was more manageable, at around $300 one way. The plan was for my uncle to loan me the rest of the money to fly from Austria to America. I didn't tell my father that the first thing I thought of wasn't geography; it was the radio. The one his brother had given him. The one that had carried news, static, music, and survival across decades. The one that was stolen, and that I had sneakily replaced. I was heading toward the source of the signal.

They say it takes a village to raise a child. In my case, it took a village to smuggle one.

At the airport, the customs officials put the first creases in my passport, turning it around in their hands, flipping pages in search of something they could not find, investigating it as if it were a foreign object.

"You say you entered Turkey from America," one official said, "but there is no stamp of entry."

Then another official chimed, "Yes, in fact, there are no stamps at all."

I fought the fear from filling my eyes, and kept my breath at bay, casually producing the police report. "My passport was stolen," I said, unfolding the paper. "This passport is my replacement."

They paused and consulted each other in Turkish, giving me sideways glances, causing my heart to beat the way it had on the bus to Ankara. After a few strikes on their keyboard, without further questions or problems, they waved me through after the thud of the first stamp graced the pages of my new passport.

Over the phone with my father, while waiting at the gate, I could hardly contain myself from sharing a laugh about my near miss at the airport. He was relieved and promised to call my uncle in Austria about my arrival time. Vienna served merely as a layover destination; upon landing, I met an uncle whom I only knew through pictures and stories. Shortly after arrival, my uncle and I rushed straight to the international airline counter, where we discovered an intriguing quirk: Round-trip tickets to Washington, DC, via JFK, were actually cheaper than one-way fares. With that $770 ticket in my hand, I was ready to start the final leg of my journey on Delta Airlines Flight 85.

My first transatlantic flight had been when I was only three months old, when my parents moved back to Iran to serve their homeland. Austria to JFK for a plane change to DC's Washington National Airport, would be the longest flight I had ever taken, and in my mind, it felt less like a flight and more like crossing an ocean by sheer will. Inside the airplane—between the engine roar, the announcements over the loudspeaker, and the constant motion—understanding the flight crew felt impossible. Add to that a very Persian reflex: Don't inconvenience anyone. Don't ask for extra. Don't draw attention to yourself. Don't cause trouble. Don't be "that person."

I could be hungry, but I convinced myself it would be too much to ask for food. So, when the flight attendants came by, I stayed polite, reserved, and kept declining refreshments and meals—only to watch the passengers around me happily eating and drinking as if this were a flying restaurant. Eventually thirst won. I finally gathered the courage and asked the flight attendant for a 7UP.

She looked at me and said, "Sprite okay?"

I froze.

Sprite? I had never heard of Sprite. I didn't know if it was another soda or a strange American word with a hidden meaning. So I did the most comfortable thing possible without sounding like I didn't understand: "I'll just take water."

After a couple of cups of water, my bladder began to protest. But by then, we were close to landing, and I decided it wasn't worth learning a whole new world—plane bathrooms—at the last minute. I told myself I could hold it. I sat there resisting, negotiating, bargaining with my own body…until we finally landed at JFK.

But that wasn't a wise move, because I hadn't accounted for US Customs and Border Protection. Before I could use a bathroom, I needed to wait in line. Two labels split the room: US Citizens/Permanent Residents and Visitors. For a second, my body moved before my brain toward the visitors' lane. Then I remembered Ankara and how I had stood in a line of Iranian visa hopefuls waiting for permission to enter, only to be told, "You're American. Go to the front."

I took a breath and stepped into the citizens' line. Long serpentine lines slowly progressing forward were marked by unintelligible chatter from fellow travelers and occasional commands from customs officers sternly directing people. Complaints about the wait drifted through the line, parents shushing restless children, teenagers grumbling about being hungry…I smiled at how familiar it all felt, no matter the country. When it was finally my turn, an officer waved me over.

"Next."

I handed over my passport and immediately had to remind myself to look up. Old habits die hard. In Iran, eye contact invited trouble from the vultures. Here, avoiding it might look suspicious. So I met the agent's eyes, even though it felt like my heart was beating far louder than the cries of the overtired babies.

He flipped through my passport, typed something into his computer.

"Where are you arriving from?"

"Turkey."

"How long were you there?"

"Ten days."

"Traveling alone?"

"Yes."

He glanced at me again, just briefly, then back to the screen. More typing.

"Anything to declare?"

"No."

A stamp hit the page. He slid the passport back under the glass.

"Welcome home."

The gravitas of the moment was trumped by the weight of my bladder. I sprinted into the terminal in search of relief before making my connection to DC. And that's when the next culture shock hit. American bathrooms had no privacy. There were gaps above and below the stall door. And worse—there was an actual vertical space near the door where anyone could peek inside. I felt exposed, almost violated by architecture. I had never used a bathroom where I felt like I might be watched. And here's the strange part: Despite the overwhelming urgency, my body refused to cooperate.

I stood there, tense and frozen, unable to initiate a stream—as if my nervous system had declared the environment unsafe and shut everything down. I closed my eyes, focused, forced calm into my muscles, and finally, mercifully, succeeded. But the surprises weren't over. Once I felt comfortable enough to sit to also have a bowel movement, I faced the final American revelation: There was no water hose. No bidet. No way to clean up except…tissue? Back in Iran, every bathroom had either a water hose, or at a minimum, a water jug—*something*—so that a person could properly clean after using the toilet. Toilet paper was for drying, not for cleaning. And that simply made sense. If any other body part became soiled, no one would consider it "clean" by merely wiping it with tissue. Water came first. Tissue came after. I couldn't imagine this was on purpose, so I figured out of all the bathrooms in JFK, I must have chosen the faulty one. The broken one. The stall where the water hose hadn't been installed yet.

But after I wasted nearly half a roll of toilet paper and still felt dirty and uneasy, I walked out and checked the other bathrooms…and then the next one…and then the next. None of them had washing capacity. I stood there, processing something far bigger than plumbing. I washed my hands, walked out of that restroom feeling strangely separated from the world around me, and looked at the sea of travelers moving in every direction. People heading to gates, dragging luggage, talking casually, eating pretzels, sipping coffee—so normal, so relaxed. And I remember thinking, half horrified and half amazed: *Do all these people have dirty bottoms…and it doesn't bother them in the slightest?*

For as long as I could remember, I had written the same word on every form I'd ever filled out: *Birthplace—New York.* It was a fact I carried without feeling, a line of ink that never came with an image. Now here I was, standing in JFK, and I tried to feel something. Pride. Recognition. Belonging. Instead, it just felt like an airport—overcrowded, loud, and relentless. People rushed past me in every direction, impatient, distracted, utterly unconcerned with the significance I had imagined this moment might hold. And then, absurdly, my mind went back to the bathrooms. All these people moving through the world so confidently, were carrying on with their day with nothing more than toilet paper.

CHAPTER 11

I had crossed an ocean, but the heat followed me to my final destination. Washington, DC, in August felt like the air had been pulled tight around me, as if the city were slowly vacuum-sealing everything that moved. On our descent into DC, from the airplane window, I spotted shapes I recognized from textbooks and television—the Washington Monument piercing the sky like a needle, tall and white, and farther off, the low, massive geometry of the Pentagon, stretching wide and confident across the landscape. These were not just buildings. They were symbols of a country that expected to be here tomorrow, and the next day, and the next. There were no giant portraits of the Imam staring down from walls and billboards, no daily reminders of who ruled and who must obey. The monuments here felt like bookmarks in time, of chapters closed, so the stories of others like me could be written.

My first chapter as an American would be written in Maryland, living with my aunt, my mother's older sister, who was also a pediatrician. Hers would be the next pair of hands to carry me forward. How many had already carried me this far? How many people had served as passports long before the document in my pocket ever did—friends, relatives, strangers, and strangers who became friends. Each had stamped my passage forward with small, cumulative acts: bowls of soup, quiet loans, borrowed courage, calculated risks, schemes whispered, and pivots made just in time.

My cousin Shahin was at the gate to greet me. He seemed to run on a higher voltage of electricity. He was a decade older than me but moved like someone who had already conquered the world, fast and confident, talking with his hands, ushering me out the door like a new school friend excited to show me the playground.

"Wow, you're tall, but I'm taller," he said, and gave me a bear hug. His grin was infectious, and while I only knew him as the static star of his wedding video, I felt an instant connection.

Exiting the airport wasn't much different than Tehran, with its cacophony of sirens, cicadas, and traffic. It was only the languages I couldn't yet separate from one another.

"First thing," he said, tossing my suitcase into the back of his pickup truck, "you should get a job. And you'll enroll in community college. It's right near the house."

He said it the way you'd say, "We should grab lunch."

I stared at him, jet-lagged, underdressed, still translating half my thoughts before I spoke them. School? Enrollment? I had no transcripts, no records, and barely enough English to argue with a cashier, let alone a registrar.

But Shahin's certainty was the same confidence I had seen in Ankara, watching American tourists stride through streets with backpacks and guidebooks, assuming the world would open when they knocked. I had wondered what it felt like to move through life that way, to expect doves instead of vultures. Now, with the help of my aunt and cousin, I would find out.

Shahin's pickup truck was immaculate. He'd rented it as part of his move abroad; he and his German wife planned on moving together to Switzerland, so they needed to clear out his old condo before leaving. He asked if I'd mind helping him move some furniture from his condo in Rockville. I thought he meant after I ate and unpacked, but he meant right now. Although I was feeling exhausted from the long flight and jet lag was beginning to take its toll, I agreed, and we set off.

As we drove to his place, Shahin explained that most of his furniture had already been moved; however, some heavier items like dressers and bed frames remained. These needed to be disassembled and loaded onto his truck. Meanwhile, his phone kept ringing; each time, it was my aunt reminding us that dinner was ready. She seemed more and more frustrated that Shahin had taken me to his old condo so quickly after I arrived.

Until the moment I met her in the kitchen that smelled like a feast, my aunt Nahid, too, had only existed to me as grainy VHS footage from Shahin's wedding. She was a face that had flickered on a television screen. We didn't look alike. But she smiled like my mother; with the same pensive tilt of the head and a similar far-off look that swept her away in deep thought. She embraced me in a way that said, "Eat, and then we have work to do."

She was a physician, like my mother, like my grandfather, and great uncle before her—another link in a chain of white coats and late nights and of belief in science and service. I had come chasing higher education and landed in a home that already spoke my language of ambition. And we would indeed get right to work.

I was given an enrollment application at Frederick Community College. One of the requirements was to provide proof of high school completion. I was sure they would reject my application without this critical document. After all, even though I had graduated as the top student in my class, my high school had not released my diploma, pending clarification on entering a university or signing up for mandatory military service. I explained this in Persian to Shahin, who relayed the story to the woman at the admissions counter. She asked us to sit and wait to meet Jim Holton, the Dean of Admissions.

I feared the meeting would end abruptly, and I would be denied an education again. My experience with any authority figure in Iran typically ended in denials and rigid negative responses. I braced myself for the worst despite Shahin's reassurances. A door opened, and a middle-aged man with salt-and-pepper hair and mustache emerged. He sat close to Shahin and me as casual as a friend, unlike the Ministry of Education official who told my father not to touch his desk because he was "untouchable refuse." Shahin shared my story of being smuggled over the mountains due to persecution and denial of access to education just days before and how I had no access to my records. I could follow his eloquent English as he spoke of *transcripts* and *diplomas* and wished I could have the ability to speak like that. Dean Holton listened attentively and graciously, keeping his eyes on me even as Shahin told the story on my behalf. He spoke *to* me, not *about* me, and I remember feeling dignified because of it.

Dean Holton asked if I would be willing to write down what I said to him on a piece of paper while handing me a blank page. I nodded and with Shahin's help, wrote a paragraph stating why I did not have access to my high school diploma. I handed it to the Dean, and he glanced at it, and promptly handed it back.

My heart raced again as he said, "You forgot to sign and date it." Breathing a sigh of relief, I signed it and handed it back. He said he would place my statement in my admissions file in lieu of my high school diploma.

I looked at Shahin puzzled and asked, "What's 'in lieu'?"

With us in tow, Dean Holton proceeded to the registrar's office and advised the lady at the counter to mark me as an "in-state" student even though I had not been in Maryland for a year. He said he did this because of my limited means.

With swagger and vigor, Dean Holton said, "Get this young man registered for his courses." Then he walked away.

I was a stranger to this man. I could have been lying. Yet he was possessed by an optimism and charity that I was quickly learning was unique to the American people. I had no tangible evidence of my records, yet he judged my sincerity. I thought of Lucy from the US embassy in Ankara. She, too, took me for my word, dignified me, and made waves to help me survive my plight. Lucy had provided me with a physical passport; however, soon people like Dean Holton would become metaphorical ones, opening doors for me, creating opportunities to help me realize my dream of becoming a doctor. This was a first for me, but I began to see I wasn't a first for them.

In Iran, physical records were a passport to education. In America, my word had become my passport.

After enrollment, I needed to take a placement test in math and English, which was an eventful mix of excitement and anxiety as I prepared for this four-hour exam. Results indicated I excelled at mathematics but needed improvement in English, which consequently required me to enroll in remedial courses.

* * *

Life with my aunt in Frederick was filled with new beginnings and familiar comforts. Her home, filled with Persian rugs and the aroma of traditional Iranian cuisine, was an inviting reminder of where I grew up. In Iran, I always knew where I wasn't allowed to go. In Maryland, I didn't know where to begin. On the streets, I heard languages I couldn't place, saw tourists unfolding maps, teenagers arguing about music, office workers half asleep and half rushing, women in business suits and sneakers, running for a cab. No one looked like they belonged more than anyone else. Everyone spoke faster than my textbooks. Slang ruled. I could understand every word in a sentence and still miss the meaning entirely. It seemed everything required the response of "Totally!" "Lame," "Sweet," or "You're killing me," which were literal to me for far too long, as were "Get out!" "Fresh," and the ever-confusing "Phat."

At a restaurant, I looked at the server with complete seriousness and asked for a "baggy dog." She smiled and brought a box for the food, explaining that I probably meant a "doggie bag."

Admittedly, the cultural differences—and the shock of entirely new routines—turned even the simplest errands into sociological adventures. Teachers invited me to call them by their first names. Between classes, boys and girls sat together on lawns smoking cigarettes, and men played football (which I had to learn to call soccer) with their shirts off—in public! Similarly, women thought nothing of sunbathing on a park bench, removing clothing as the sun heated up their skin.

The "supermarket," a word and a concept that never existed in Iran in my time, stretched on forever. Aisles of cereal and milk that felt excessive to someone raised on daily bread runs and small bakeries owned by people we knew by name. I didn't know cereal could come in so many varieties and competing brands, and I was confused as to how bread stayed fresh inside suffocating plastic bags held closed by twist ties.

From payphones, you could hear people speaking freely; my aunt's answering machine played back messages without codes or caution, trusting that no one was listening. Even the way Americans wore their clothes—bright, casual, with words spread across them—billboards of their values and opinions. Zippered jogging suits that both men and women wore when they weren't exercising looked like a national uniform.

Here, ambulances were just ambulances, not portable prisons disguised as ambulances. Their sirens wailed to save you, not to enslave you. Music was everywhere in 1994. Loud. Public. Proud. My cousin took me to a record store—a real one, with glass windows and posters tacked to the walls—and I froze in the doorway. Rows and rows of CDs, whole sections labeled *Rock*, *Hip-Hop*, *R&B*. Kids stood in line buying Green Day and moms bought Boys II Men. No one whispering. No one watching. No one selling or buying music like it was an illegal drug. People waited in line overnight for concert tickets, and new albums "dropped" (another new slang term for me) at midnight, where a party in the street broke out outside Sam Goody while fans waited for the doors to unlock.

And then I saw Persian albums produced in Los Angeles. Right there on the shelf. Ebi. Andy & Kouros. Voices I had only known through fuzzy bootleg tapes suddenly stared back at me in glossy color. I kept waiting for someone to pull me aside and ask what I was doing, but the only question was, "Cash or credit?"

On the radio, it was Nirvana and Tupac and voices that sounded angry, playful, fearless. My cousin flipped stations like it was nothing, like he owned the air itself. They called some music "grunge"; their leading man, Kurt Cobain, had died months earlier. I filled in the gaps of pop culture when I could. East Coast versus West Coast, Mariah Carey as pop princess, Michael Jackson as Elvis's son-in-law while still being the King of Pop. Back in Iran, we listened quietly, always with one ear tuned to the door. Here, music made headlines and doubled as soap operas that rivaled the most famous novellas in Iran.

I learned how to be young in America through television archetypes. The message was "life here is light." *The Fresh Prince of Bel-Air* said, "America is loud and expressive." I didn't have too much free time, but in 1994, everyone stopped for "Must-See TV." In Iran, everything was Must-Not-See. Here, we watched twenty-somethings hang around in coffee shops, Seinfeld ruminate about "nothing," and doctoring in an *ER* that looked very different from how medicine was administered in Iran. Before professors began lectures, classmates talked about *90210*, an indulgent show about teens, dating, cars, and fashion, which was a total culture shock for someone raised with gender segregation, modesty, and parental control. *The X-Files* fascinated me. Not just because of the show's science fiction base, but for its outward expression of government distrust and dark humor, which strangely hit close to home. I remembered the adults, including my father, giving funny and ominous nicknames to Iran's leaders, creating puns about the government's incompetencies, to secretly blow off steam. Here, the more steam that was blown, the higher the ratings. There were the talk shows, too, with which I was familiar through satellite TV in Iran, but the wilder and more entertaining ones aired in the afternoon back-to-back: Ricki Lake and Jerry Springer. I was fascinated by how, after a show publicly displaying the darkest secrets of couples being confronted in a public forum, Jerry would have his final thoughts with elevated words and sincerity, as if none of the conflict affected him in the least.

Aside from the lifestyle adjustments, Shahin helped me complete several logistical and procedural errands and paperwork tasks to establish my new life in America: financial aid forms, opening a bank account, getting a social security card, getting a driver's license, and navigating the neighborhood. Each task represented a small victory toward building my life here; each was another step closer.

Shortly after I arrived at my aunt Nahid's home in Maryland, a relative of her late husband also moved in the basement in the room next to me. His name was Shahram, and his family lived in China. He was about to start his master's program at American University. He was generally English speaking; Persian was not his strong suit. He became a critical presence in my life as he helped proofread my essays, improve my conversational English, and become a portal to his social contacts. We would play backgammon at night and speak of life, education, aspirations, and of course, girls. With an easygoing demeanor and English proficiency that was invaluable for me, I admired and attempted to emulate Shahram's ability to charm people effortlessly, an art he demonstrated admirably by chatting up girls with ease. I used my attempt at edgy cool expression back then to describe him, saying, "Shahram can get his 'mack' on girls very well."

Living with my aunt who was a busy founding partner in Frederick Pediatric Associates—the largest pediatric group in Frederick, Maryland—meant she wasn't always around the household, making Shahram the main person I practiced speaking

English with. When I had essays or papers to be proofread and edited, I would bring them to him. Being someone who studied the humanities with an emphasis on international peace and conflict resolution, Shahram was adept with words: I remembered him being eloquent yet patient enough when I said something wrong. He'd quickly correct me, saying, "Well, you can't say it that way; instead, you need to say it like this."

Securing financial aid proved to be one of the most daunting tasks. I filled out the required FAFSA form at the small dining table in my aunt's house, hunched over papers that might as well have been written in code. Income. Assets. Tax forms. Words I barely understood in English, and even if I did, I hadn't lived long enough to put them into practice. Shahram translated when I got stuck, explaining what I didn't know to ask.

"So they just…give you money?" I asked him.

He shrugged. "Yeah. If you qualify."

Qualify. The irony was so thick it made me laugh quietly. In Iran, I had qualified for nothing except rejection. We dropped the envelope in the mailbox, and I tried not to think about it. I had learned that hope was dangerous when you depended on institutions. A few weeks later, another envelope arrived. It was thick and stamped with words that seemed surreal: US Department of Education.

My hands shook as I opened it. Inside was an award letter for a Pell Grant for an amount that would be enough to cover my tuition and some expenses, like books. For US citizens who fall below a certain income stream, the Pell Grant is not a loan to be paid back. It was as if they were going to pay me to go to school. I read the letter again, afraid I had mistranslated the meaning.

Shahram leaned over my shoulder. "See? I told you."

But I wasn't listening to him. I was staring at my name, and all I could think of was how I would pay it back. Maybe not in money itself, but by becoming a doctor and healing people and giving back to the community that had immediately and without question lifted me up.

And suddenly, the gravitas of my American passport gained momentum. The secret that had been sewn into my clothes, beating like a heart inside a shoe box, was now powerful and visible. This money, this opportunity, which stated in black and white, "you are eligible," existed because I was a citizen. Because before I was even conceived, my parents had insisted on giving me choices. In Iran, I had been erased from the system and didn't even qualify to have access to my own transcripts, while in a few weeks in America, I had been entered into it.

I began to understand just how deeply education—and its absence—had shaped the world I came from. Those who had managed to become doctors or professionals had done so before the Islamic Revolution; they were already middle-aged or older. There were almost no young physicians, no emerging generation stepping into those roles. It was as if an entire cohort had been quietly erased before it had the chance to begin.

It became clear that this was not accidental. The policy to ban Bahá'ís from higher education was deliberate: to ensure that they would never become part of the educated class, never hold positions of influence, never help shape the intellectual or professional future of their own country. Over time, that kind of exclusion does more than limit opportunity; it narrows imagination. When education is denied long enough, even the idea of possibility begins to fade.

And yet, not long after arriving, I encountered something that challenged that narrative. At a gathering of my aunt Nahid's colleagues at Frederick Pediatric Associates, I met a young Bahá'í man in his early thirties who was already a practicing pediatrician. Until that moment, I had never seen someone from our community so young in that role. It felt almost unreal.

In seeing him, I understood that what had been impossible in Iran was not truly impossible—it had simply been forbidden.

That night, I lay awake thinking about BIHE, about teachers risking prison, about motorbikes carrying homework through back alleys, about students memorizing lessons in living rooms because classrooms were forbidden to them. And here I was, eighteen years old, legally invited to walk into them. Back home, I had seen what "brain drain" really meant—the steady loss of gifted people from a country that could have thrived on the brilliance of its people had it not driven them away. I pondered that the true infrastructure of a nation was not its oil fields and roads and bridges. It was its brilliant minds who had left en masse.

Now, I was becoming part of that loss.

CHAPTER 12

The first time I walked into a classroom at the community college was without ceremony. It was just a room with fluorescent lights, rows of desks, no images of a Supreme Leader, and a chalkboard that didn't carry slogans or threats. Students drifted in, backpacks slung over one shoulder, complaining about homework and arguing about where to eat later. I took a seat near the middle of the room—close enough to hear but far enough not to be noticed—and placed my notebook on the desk. The first time a professor entered the classroom, I leaped to my feet in respect, only to find that I was the only one who stood. I proceeded to sit down and pretended all was well. The professor nodded and started teaching. No declarations. No oaths. No loyalty tests disguised as morning rituals.

Instructors were exceptionally supportive, particularly Mary, my remedial English teacher, who offered me extra help during her office hours so I could progress more quickly. I was determined to move up to English 101 after just one semester of introductory courses. She initially had reservations but eventually agreed to let me take a test to demonstrate my readiness. After dedicating hours to memorizing and writing a research paper with the help of Shahram on "hypermedia learning," I took the test. I passed it, earning myself a place in English 101!

For the first time, I was immersed in a classroom where differences weren't hidden or punished. My classmates were American, Russian, Romanian, Indonesian—each carrying their own accents, food, holidays, and histories. In Iran, diversity existed, of course, but it lived in the shadows. Officially, we were meant to be one thing, believe one thing, and worship one way.

Shahram and I would talk for hours into the night about his own experiences as a student. He took time to explain various cultural nuances to help me acclimate to life in the US. These conversations included everyday etiquette, like the importance of small talk, which was not common in Iran. He also discussed classroom norms, such as the expectation to participate actively in discussions and the more casual interactions between students and professors compared to the formal respect shown to teachers back home. Shahram's advice was invaluable, providing insights I couldn't have gained by reading books or brochures alone.

Slowly, I began to settle in and made friends with students who were eager to understand my background and help me adapt. Some of us formed study groups, shared meals, and explored the campus. There were moments of homesickness for my best friend, Babak, teasing my sister on her birthday for being so "old," and the smell of my father's newspapers, and there were times when I felt overwhelmed by cultural differences and academic workload. Yet, each time these feelings surfaced, I reminded myself why I came to America, the opportunities ahead, and the support I received from my cousin and new friends. As my confidence grew, so did my nerve to date.

I met Nikki from Baku, Azerbaijan, while at community college. We soon became close. Back then, if you wanted to impress somebody, you would create a song mix and record it on a cassette or burn it onto a CD. The time, energy, and curation served as tokens of affection, as the music communicated what you couldn't or what you didn't have the guts to say out loud. So, that's what I did to let Nikki know I liked her. I made her a mix tape. It worked and I had my very first date. Considering our financial limitations, dinner at Olive Garden, with its all-you-can-eat salad and breadsticks, was classy enough.

I didn't really know how people dated. What I knew about romance came from stealing kisses with my older neighbor who lived a floor above me in Tehran. I gleaned much of it from the movies I loved and from taking note of what upset and pleased my mother and sister. I had never learned how to walk up to a girl, ask her out, flirt openly, or sit across a table and talk about the weather. If I had stayed in Iran, I sometimes wondered if I would still be waiting for permission to experience the innocent exhilaration of a girl making eye contact—or if I would have already been married, following a script I never wrote.

So when Nikki entered my life, everything felt new and unsteady and thrilling all at once. She worked as an au pair and lived with the family, which made our dating life a little complicated. We couldn't exactly announce ourselves at the front door, so I would sometimes sneak in through a window from the backyard that opened into her basement room. It felt like I was still carrying the habits of secrecy with me, except this somehow felt fun. Nikki had a lightness about her, a laugh that came easily, and a way of believing in the future that felt contagious. She talked about building a life in America and helping her parents and sister immigrate someday. She was already planning forward, while I was still learning how to stand still in the present.

One night, we sat on the stoop of the home she lived in, sharing fries from a paper bag, looking up at the stars. Nothing dramatic was happening. No danger. No hiding in stairwells. No one was being carried away by a van. And it hit me—this was what being a teenager was supposed to feel like. Ordinary, and even a little boring. *Safe.* I remember thinking how strange it was that something so simple could feel like a miracle.

I went on dates with one or two other girls around that time, but nothing had the closeness I felt with Nikki, as we had a genuine attraction. We also related to one another after growing up with political upheaval, living under an oppressive government system, being shaped by politics neither of us had chosen, and spending our childhoods wishing on stars. I didn't share with her how I thought about her ten-year-old face staring at the very same time and at the very same comet I had made promises to, but I was awed by the image. With Nikki, I didn't just learn how to be with someone; I learned how to relate, how to listen, and how to cherish what could happen between people in the quiet. It felt like growing up at double speed.

* * *

Shahram was the first to say what everyone was thinking: I needed a job if I was going to support myself and keep up with community college. Tuition was one thing, but dates to Olive Garden and a growing social life demanded a supplemental income. By 1995, I felt just acclimated enough to try my luck. There was one place that seemed to be hiring every human being in America, so I applied there. That's how I became an employee earning $4.25 an hour and officially entered the American workforce, one Big Mac at a time.

As my English was limited, I wasn't allowed to work the register at McDonald's; instead, I was assigned to the grill and fry stations. My initial task was mastering patty-making: placing nine frozen patties onto a grill, lowering its top, pressing a timer, and moving them into warmer bins. We were supposed to throw away any unused patties after thirty minutes. However, I soon discovered some coworkers reset the timers without ever making fresh ones; my first lesson in workplace shortcuts.

Working at the fry station was a bit more challenging. Dropping frozen fries in metal baskets into hot oil caused small oil splatters that occasionally popped on my hands, leaving scars I still have. Regardless, I took great pride in learning the ropes while expanding my English by engaging with both coworkers and customers alike. Every interaction, be it at the college, at work, on dates, or with the Bahá'í youth Shahram introduced me to, was an opportunity to learn and improve my English.

I would come across new words and definitions every day. There was a long mirror next to my bed at my aunt's house. I would write a word on the front of a Post-it note and its meaning on the back and stick it to my mirror. I would not remove any note until I felt I had mastered the word. There were times when the entire mirror was obscured by my notes. This would create an extra incentive to master more words so I could remove the notes one at a time and be able to see my own face in the mirror. Sometimes, I would get excited about a new word I learned and would totally blow it when trying to use it.

I took a girl to Applebee's one evening and, in my attempt at the art of small talk, said, "Isn't this the most effervescent evening?" She looked at me like I was crazy. So much for trying to impress her.

I'll never forget Mr. Louis, my manager at McDonald's. His size and presence caused some uneasiness within me; nonetheless, he always kept an air of authority while remaining polite but strict with us all. Although to me he was always "Mr. Louis," many other employees referred to him as simply "Louis," something which took some getting used to for me.

As my English improved, it felt like time to move on to better opportunities. So I did what I had been trained to do my entire life when leaving any position, no matter how small: I wrote a formal resignation letter.

I typed it carefully on my cousin's old Mac, thanking McDonald's for the opportunity to work, expressing my gratitude for the experience, and wishing the company continued success in all future endeavors. You would have thought I was resigning from the presidency, not the patty station. But in my mind, you did not simply quit a job. You explained yourself and showed respect. You closed the door properly, while leaving a bridge as golden as the arches I was leaving behind.

I handed the letter to Mr. Louis. He skimmed it for about three seconds, looked up at me, and said, "Okay."

Just...okay.

No handshake. No "We'll miss you." Not even a "Good luck." I learned that in America, even your exits could be as fast as its food.

My step up the employment ladder meant a return to my roots as a tutor. The experience I had was with high school kids, but I had a knack for explaining concepts in a way that was understandable. It was a communication skill I was happy to exercise in a world where I found it difficult to communicate. I was really lucky to land a tutoring gig through the college's work-study program, and while it was helping me tremendously to stay afloat, I felt needed and helpful, a contribution I could make that was equal to the payment I received. This job not only paid more than McDonald's at $6.00 per hour, but it also kept me engaged with subjects I loved.

Maddie Remsburg was an energetic, petite woman with short hair who welcomed me with open arms into the tutorial office. I told her about my desire to become a tutor and my experience back in Iran. "Great," was her response when I told her I could tutor physics, math, algebra, and calculus.

One of my favorite parts of the work-study program was holding office hours in the tutoring center. I had to be there during my assigned window, whether anyone showed up or not. Sometimes students had appointments. Other times, no one came at all, and I would sit alone at the desk, waiting, studying, the clock ticking. But even on those quiet days, something had shifted. For the first time in my life, the tables felt turned. I wasn't the kid trying to stay invisible. I was the one behind the desk. The one people were sent to for help. An authority—however small, however temporary—on subjects I loved and understood.

Back home, knowing you were good at something wasn't always safe to celebrate. Academic pride was complicated for me. In my case, it had been interrupted altogether. With an undiagnosed learning disability as a child, I had spent years wondering whether I was different. Even when I became one of the top students in my grade, there had been no ceremony for it, no public acknowledgment from the other teachers, kids, or parents. I had experienced no graduation ceremonies, no caps and gowns, no valedictorians or salutatorians, and no plaques or honors or Dean's lists while I climbed the academic ladder through high school. Achievement was so quiet it ceased to exist. So sitting there, getting paid to wait in case someone needed *me*, felt almost unreal. And then students started asking for me by name. That part stunned me.

"Is Nizam here today?"

"Can I wait for him?"

It wasn't just flattering; it was reinforcing. One afternoon, a student came in completely lost in calculus, which was my favorite subject. We worked problem after problem, erasing and rewriting, chasing understanding one derivative at a time. What was supposed to be a short session turned into many sessions. The next week, he came back grinning. He had passed his exam.

What I liked most about tutoring wasn't really the math. It was sitting with people who felt overwhelmed and helping them realize the problem in front of them was smaller than it appeared. Most students didn't come in saying, "I don't understand this formula." They came in carrying fear of failing the exam, of falling behind, or that maybe they just weren't smart enough. Once we slowed things down and broke the problems into pieces, I could almost see their shoulders drop as panic gave way to focus. I had seen this many times before, in many places.

I had watched my parents and other BIHE teachers do this constantly, without titles or paychecks. In living rooms turned into classrooms, in borrowed spaces where young people gathered with notebooks and nerves, I saw how much of teaching was really about helping students believe they could keep going. At my home, I saw the same thing in my mother's makeshift medical office with parents arriving late at night with feverish children, broken bones, test results they didn't understand, and worst-case scenarios already playing in their heads. Before she ever examined the patient, my mother examined the fear. She listened, explained, and reassured. Only then did the medicine begin to matter. I think that's where I learned that helping someone often starts with helping them exhale. I had my own way of doing that. I liked to make people laugh, and I love to laugh myself. Humor was my shortcut to calm and a way to break tension when everything felt too heavy. Even in tutoring sessions, a corny joke at the right moment could loosen the knot in someone's stomach enough for them to think clearly.

I wasn't interested in education as a career, but I was very interested in that space between confusion and understanding—the trust it takes for someone to admit they're stuck, and the relief that comes when someone stays long enough to help. It made me think about care in a broader sense in that helping someone isn't just a technical skill, but one that requires presence, empathy, and the willingness to stay. I decided that medicine for me would not be just about anatomy and labs. I would meet people at the exact moment they were afraid, confused, or stuck, and help them find their footing again. The white coat might change, the setting might change, but the work would be the same kind I had already been practicing: earning trust, easing fear, and connecting through laughter and shared humanity. The best physicians, after all, must be educators first. Those who take the time to explain to a patient the reason why they feel a particular way or the mechanism of their illness or injury or the reason for the medicines you are prescribing, are more likely to have patients who are adherent and compliant to the care and have the best outcomes. The ability to teach became the underpinning of my dream to be a compassionate doctor.

Within six months, I received my first raise. My pay increased from $6.00 an hour to $7.00, which felt like a significant achievement. I remember a letter from my father calling me the equivalent of "money bags," but I could sense he was very proud of me, for not only surviving but thriving in my new world. I began to think like Nikki, imagining me becoming the source of a path for immigration for my own family.

Additionally, my tutoring job provided a sense of community. Through meeting other tutors and staff members, I formed friendships and connections that enriched my college experience. We would often share stories and tips, providing support as we navigated balancing work and studies together.

It is strange to say, but the same forces that isolated us in Iran also forged a closeness I feel lucky to have had. Exclusion pushed us inward, and in that shrinking space we built something fierce and intimate—a community bound not only by belief, but by shared fear, shared resilience, and a thousand crafty workarounds that kept life moving. That kind of belonging grows when people depend on one another.

When I left, I didn't just leave a country; I left a safety net and the certainty that no matter what happened, there were people who knew my story and would show up without being asked. In America, I had freedom, but I had to learn how to build belonging instead of inheriting it. The more I found the courage to put myself out there, the more I began to assemble a community of my own making, not born of necessity, but of choice.

The capitalist in me began to come out. I liked having money in my pocket and realized it was another kind of passport in this country obsessed with consumption. I decided to take on a second job as a delivery driver for Papa John's. The flexible hours worked perfectly with my school schedule. While this job only paid $5.50 an hour compared to tutoring's $7.00, the cash tips more than compensated. I could make between $12.00 and $13.00 an hour, which made a huge difference in my income.

This meant I needed to buy a car. Mr. Rahmi, a friend of my aunt's, owned a small dealership in West Virginia, and he helped me purchase a used car for $2,500 at his shop. It worked just fine and featured my very first automatic transmission. My left foot kept searching for a clutch that didn't exist, muscle memory refusing to let go. Back in Tehran, driving meant constant shifting, constant attention. Here, the car did the work for me. Just press and go.

My Ford Taurus was an '88, navy blue, and ordinary to everyone else, but I had bought it with my own hard-earned money, and that made it extraordinary to me. It felt like proof that I was learning how to move forward in a country that, finally, seemed to be moving with me instead of ahead of me.

I still remember my first encounter with Papa John's manager, Dale. He was a big guy with a large belly who was content to sit in the back office ordering people around. Navigating my way around town as a pizza deliveryman required me to study a giant map on the wall at my store to memorize routes and write down addresses as best as I could remember them. One particularly cold night during Super Bowl weekend, Dale begged me to work, promising it would be a lucrative night.

As I set off with three pizzas to deliver to a wealthy home, the weather became hazardous, with slick ice covering every surface. I finally reached the house, got out with pizzas in my hand, and slipped on the icy sidewalk. I landed hard on my tailbone, and the pizzas flew into the air. Only one managed to remain intact.

Despite the pain, I picked myself up, grabbed the surviving pizza, and hobbled to the door. A woman opened it, and I could see the guests behind her, eagerly awaiting their food. "We ordered three pizzas," she said, her eyes narrowing at the single box in my hands.

"I'm so sorry," I explained. "I slipped on the ice and fell. Here's one of your pizzas. I'll go back to the store and get the other two remade. Please call the store and let them know what happened so they can prepare the replacements."

She wasn't pleased but agreed to call. I made my painful way back to the car and drove back to the store. By the time I got there, Dale was fuming. "You lost the pizzas?" he shouted, eyeing my shoes as if they were to blame. "Look at those shoes. No tread at all. What were you thinking?"

I tried to explain, but he wasn't in the mood to listen. He begrudgingly made the new pizzas and handed them to me without another word. I returned to the house, delivered the pizzas, and, unsurprisingly, received no tip. When I got back to the store, the night wasn't over yet. It was busy, and there were more deliveries to be made.

Dale, however, decided that any tips given to the restaurant that night wouldn't be shared with me. I didn't know enough about labor laws to contest his decision. Nor did I know that the woman's driveway should've been salted and that I could've held her liable for my fall, especially if I had suffered an injury. I was sore, both physically and emotionally, and decided then and there that it would be my last night delivering pizzas. This time, I did not write a formal resignation letter. "I quit" was all I could muster with anger as I walked out. For years, I kept the bright red Papa John's jacket in my closet. It was a reminder to me of my humble beginnings and of how I would never treat other people. It had been a year of firsts, but I had decided that when it came to being mistreated and disrespected, Dale would be a last.

CHAPTER 13

Those two years at community college were built on grit and repetition—long days, longer nights, and the quiet discipline of showing up. Every semester brought new cultural adjustments and academic hurdles, but instead of wearing me down, each one seemed to fortify me in ways I hadn't known I was capable of. I was no longer just surviving; I was living fully.

One of the turning points came when my math professor, Anne Committo, urged me to enter the American Mathematical Association of Two-Year Colleges competition. She saw something in me that I had not yet learned to claim for myself. Her faith became a kind of permission—to push harder, to aim higher, to imagine myself as someone who could compete. I studied late into the night, working through sample problems that usually take years of training to master, chasing patterns and proofs with the same hunger that had driven me across borders.

When the results were finally announced, I had to read them twice to believe them. First place in the Mid-Atlantic region. Seventh in the nation. It was as if Halley's Comet picked me up, threw me on her back, and let me ride with her across the universe. The recognition wasn't just a trophy or a line on a résumé;

it was confirmation that the long road, the detours, the risks, and the waiting had not been in vain.

I applied to several universities as my time at the community college was nearing its end. In the mid-1990s, information on pre-med programs wasn't at my fingertips. I had to go in pursuit of applications, information packets, opinions, and reviews. I called anyone who might help: friends of friends who had gone before me. One pointed me to Cornell, and another suggested I set my sights on the more attainable University of Maryland. I was encouraged to apply to the University of Virginia in Charlottesville by a Bahá'í medical student named Rad, who had graduated from there and was studying medicine at Johns Hopkins. Rad said that UVA had an excellent reputation as an academic powerhouse, and the pre-med students there had a higher chance of securing medical school admissions than "lesser universities."

"But don't get your hopes up, man," he said. "You aren't from Virginia, and the competition is fierce. Have a backup plan." His words reminded me of my father's words when he said, "The statistical odds are against you…"

"Applying" was anything but simple. First, you had to track down a school's contact information—often through directory assistance—then call during business hours and hope someone answered. You spelled out your name and address carefully, knowing one mistake could delay everything. Then you waited weeks for a thick application packet to arrive by mail—no tracking, no confirmation, just patience.

Filling it out required precision. I used an old typewriter, where every keystroke was permanent. There was no undo, no margin for error. And while Correcto-Type promised salvation, it mostly just spotlighted your mistake—turning a quiet typo into a bold, chalky announcement that something had gone wrong. So I worked slowly and carefully, knowing how much depended on each page.

And then came more waiting. Each day I checked the mailbox, learning to read the signals: a thin envelope meant rejection; a thick one held possibility. It was slow, uncertain, and often nerve-wracking—but it also made every step feel intentional, earned, and deeply connected to the journey.

I was accepted to all of my choices. When the University of Virginia accepted me as a transfer student, I was excited to share the news with Rad. There was another advantage to going to Charlottesville, Virginia: Dr. Kavian Milani and his wife, Leila—family friends—lived there, training for residency in family medicine. This was a source of reassurance and guidance for me, and my relationship with Kavian as a mentor and older brother blossomed.

The ceremony that would end my time at Frederick Community College took place on a bright, sunny afternoon in May of 1996. There was no one in the audience I could wave to, no arms waiting for me when I stepped off the stage. My parents were thousands of miles away, and I had learned by then that freedom often comes with empty chairs. Still, as the diploma was placed in my hands, I felt something settle inside me. No transcripts denied. No doors closed. No explanations demanded. I was doing what I had come to do, and no one could take this one away from me.

I was among a few outstanding students selected by the college president, President Betts, to address the audience. *Me?* Only two years earlier, I had been denied a voice. Nobody in authority had wanted to hear what I had to say. The system said I was not worthy of an argument or an opinion. Even when my rights were being taken from me in front of my eyes, I was denied a voice to advocate for myself, to fight back. Now, my voice was being requested.

"The world is becoming closer with the advent of the Internet," my presentation began. I spoke about global connectivity and how technology was allowing people to stay in touch and share knowledge across vast distances more easily than ever before. But for me, this wasn't theory—it was personal. Email quickly became my daily lifeline. Through it, I shared ordinary moments with my parents, learned about my sister's engagement and wedding, and stayed close to my cousins without costly international calls or the need to use the fax machine.

It amazed me how much could change in just two years. Not long before, my parents hadn't even known whether I was alive—whether I had made it across the border, whether I was safe, whether I would ever call again. Back then, news traveled slowly and painfully, like waiting for a once-in-a-lifetime comet to cross the sky and hoping you'd be there to see it. Now, with a few keystrokes, I could send proof of life across continents: *I'm here. I'm okay. I'm still moving forward.*

* * *

As I prepared to enter the University of Virginia, I felt a mix of excitement and nervousness. The university represented a significant step up from community college. The coursework would be more demanding, and the environment would be more competitive. But I was ready for the challenge. The anticipation of diving deeper into my studies, exploring new fields of knowledge, and meeting people from diverse backgrounds filled me with a sense of purpose.

I knew that the transition wouldn't be easy. There would be moments of doubt and struggle, but I felt equipped to handle them. The resilience I had built during my time at community college would serve me well. I learned to embrace challenges and to view them as opportunities for growth. This mindset would be crucial as I navigated the rigorous demands of university life.

The first days at the University of Virginia were a whirlwind of new experiences and emotions. Walking onto the sprawling campus for the first time, I was immediately struck by its sheer size and the bustling energy that seemed to permeate every corner. Coming from the smaller, more intimate environment of Frederick Community College, the University of Virginia felt like a whole new world. It represented a fresh start and a place where I could explore my academic interests more deeply and grow as an individual.

The initial excitement was quickly accompanied by a sense of trepidation. The academic environment at the university was far more demanding than anything I had experienced before. The coursework was rigorous, and the expectations were high. I attended orientation sessions and introductory classes that set the tone for the semester, and it quickly became apparent that I would need to step up my game to succeed here.

Making these adjustments was not easy, and there were moments when I felt out of my depth. However, forming new friendships in the dormitory and building a support system made a significant difference. During the first week, I met several students who were also navigating the challenges of their first semester. We bonded over shared experiences and the mutual understanding that we were all in this together.

It had taken a Bahá'í village to raise me in Iran, a village of good Samaritan strangers to smuggle me out, and now, I'd found my own village—one that would support and champion me through pre-med and usher me to medical school.

As a transfer student, I came to university life in the middle of most other students' four-year programs. When it came to joining clubs or fraternities, finding friend groups, having dormmates, I was two years behind many of the third-and-fourth year students who seemed to enjoy a campus rhythm, familiarity, and a belonging that I didn't have but very much wanted.

I lived in student housing during my junior year when word spread about the administration renaming a dormitory and designating the housing to an eclectic mix of students. Like America's great experiment of achieving a melting pot, the dorm, aptly named Mosaic House, would promote cross-cultural understanding and discourse in one living quarters. I imagined opinion and debate circling the air in the common areas, enabling students to connect and find they were more in common than they assumed. Expanding the scope of education, creating a world in which students learn much more from their personal interactions and experiences than from any book, thrilled me. I applied with hopes I would be considered.

Before I was able to unpack a box, it became apparent to me that I was among a very diverse population—LGBTQ, African American activists, politically active white students. Rich kids, poor kids, immigrants, religious people, atheists, it was truly a mosaic house. We became so close. We shared many meals together, we supported each other in our times of stress, proofed dissertations and personal statements and helped study for finals and MCATs and helped each other with mock interviews. We'd lay on top of each other platonically, watching episodes of *90210* and *Melrose Place* in the lounge, and even prank each other during commercial breaks. This was our time to discover how relatable we all were—all with parents we wanted to make proud, while grappling with our identities. We were each other's cheerleaders, sounding boards, and confessionals. This was the time in our life when our friends were our family, and Mosaic House was where this family lived.

In the halls, we would have intellectual conversations until about 3:00 a.m., right before Gumby's Pizza closed. We'd lose ourselves in our sharing, but steal ourselves just enough time to place our phone order for a few pizzas, enraging the student worker who was closing up.

We were at the forefront of creating an environment where people were honest about themselves, sharing secrets that even their parents didn't know. I came from a place that would severely persecute the LBGTQ+ community, and one of our friends came out to us, with deep trust and a relief that bonded us even more deeply.

Still learning to understand my new home country, my idea of America became one of creating environments of widely different backgrounds of people having conversations and supporting each other's growth. I shared a dorm room with Kapil, a gentle, thoughtful student of Indian descent who had grown up in Kenya. Our room was simple—just bunk beds and the rhythms of student life. Despite his fear of heights, a coin toss put him on the top bunk.

One night, he was already in bed while I studied below, my lamp clipped to the headboard. Eventually, exhaustion won. I turned off the light, and my biochemistry book slipped from my hands, hitting the floor with a dull thud.

A moment later, Kapil climbed down. I assumed he was heading out, but instead he came to my side, picked up the book, gently kissed it, and placed it on the desk.

"What did you just do?" I asked.

"You should never leave a book on the floor," he said. "It is disrespectful."

"But it's not a holy book," I said. "It's just biochemistry."

He shook his head. "All books carry knowledge. And knowledge is sacred."

There was just so much to learn in this world within a world. I never forgot that.

When good news came, the first people we wanted to tell were our friends in Mosaic House. I met a Christian girl originally from India, and I was the first person she told that she had received an admissions letter from Johns Hopkins. Invested in my success, she coached me on improving my interview questions for med school.

Forty-five of us lived there together in a milestone year of my life. I had experienced a microcosm of America by simply dorming.

When we left, we each painted a 4 x 4-inch tile and placed it onto a board. Each tile was a self-portrait to represent our backgrounds. Mine was a Bahá'í symbol. Another student from India painted an Om symbol.

Eventually, the program ended, and the name of the dorm reverted back to Hoxton. However, that art piece that we all contributed to is still there, welcoming students at the building entrance.

I immersed myself in campus activities and student organizations that enriched my university experience. I joined several clubs that fit my interests and passions. One of the first organizations I became involved with was the International Student Association. Through this association, I met people from all over the world, each with unique stories and perspectives. It was a reminder of the global community I was a part of and the importance of embracing cultural diversity.

Participating in these activities also helped me develop leadership skills and build my confidence. I took on roles within the organizations, organizing events and helping to plan activities. These experiences taught me the value of teamwork and the importance of effective communication. They also provided a break from the academic rigors, allowing me to relax and enjoy my time at the university.

Another significant aspect of my university life was involvement in the pre-med society. This group was instrumental in providing guidance and resources for students aspiring to enter medical school. Through the pre-med society, I attended workshops on medical school applications, participated in mock interviews, and received advice from older students who had successfully navigated the process. The mentorship and support from this community were crucial in helping me stay focused on my goal of becoming a physician.

In addition to these activities, I made it a point to attend various lectures and seminars hosted by the university. These events featured speakers from different fields and offered insights into a wide range of topics. They broadened my horizons and sparked new interests. I found myself drawn to subjects and disciplines that I hadn't considered before. My lens was widening, while at the same time, I felt a constant pull to stay connected not only to my studies, but to art, music, and the pieces of home that anchored my identity. That longing eventually took shape as the Persian Ensemble of Charlottesville, a small but passionate group of four: a young university faculty member who played piano, a hospital nurse specializing in infection control as a vocalist, an undergraduate who played the Persian goblet drum—the tombak—and me, serving as both vocalist and organizer.

We practiced often, in the modest home of that young engineering faculty and his wife, singing Persian folk songs accompanied by piano, tombak, and two voices. What began as a hobby quickly became something more polished. Eventually, with a mixture of pride and naïveté, we booked time at a small studio in Charlottesville, recorded a CD, and had it arranged and produced. It was far more than we expected to accomplish, and we were thrilled.

Not long after, we heard about a local radio station—The Prism—which hosted a live folk music night broadcast across Central Virginia. Without hesitation, we sent in an application under the name Persian Ensemble of Charlottesville, imagining how intriguing it might be for local audiences to hear Persian folk music alongside American folk traditions.

When the day arrived, we drove just outside Charlottesville to the station. The Prism had a modest stage, a piano, some seating—nothing extravagant—but it had an energy that hinted at history. As we walked in, our excitement turned into unease. The other performers were bluegrass musicians from the Appalachian region, dressed casually, carrying banjos, mandolins, and fiddles, sporting mullets, tattoos, and an unmistakable mountain charm with sun-kissed skin. We, on the other hand, had arrived in suits and ties, polished and formal, looking like visiting diplomats who had taken a wrong turn into a honky-tonk gathering.

We felt like misfits. While waiting for our turn, we listened to their music—raw, soulful bluegrass that filled the room with harmonies of another America. And though they were polite, we were convinced they were eyeing us as outsiders: the foreign quartet singing in a language they didn't understand, performing songs from a culture worlds away.

When our moment finally came, we stepped onto the stage, were introduced—somewhat tentatively—as the Persian Ensemble of Charlottesville—and began our set of Persian folk songs. The piano, the tombak, and our voices filled the room with a sound that belonged everywhere and nowhere all at once. We finished, stepped down, and braced ourselves for indifference.

The bluegrass musicians gathered around us, smiling, embracing us, thanking us for sharing our music. They told us how beautiful and soulful the melodies were. We, in turn, praised their music. In that small radio station in Central Virginia, where Appalachian folk met centuries-old Persian song, barriers dissolved instantly. Music—in its stubborn, generous way—did what diplomacy, language, and appearance often fail to do. It made us friends and equals. It made us belong.

* * *

I participated in a flu study at the end of my first year at UVA. It came during the summer when I was looking for ways to earn more spending money. It was then that I saw an advertisement for one. Participation required young, healthy participants without chronic illnesses to be inoculated with the influenza virus and then quarantined for eleven days in a hospital ward.

In 1997, this study paid $2250; participants inhaled the flu virus through their nose, with either placebo medication or specific treatments to monitor the illnesses progress and track the viral load in secretions. Daily nasal washings and labs would take place to collect samples for evaluation of viral load in secretions.

As soon as I signed up for the study and moved into the hospital for its duration, I instructed my dorm roommate to make up excuses if my parents called, for example, saying I was out of town but not mentioning I was at a hospital. There were no cell phones then, and calling internationally from the hospital landline was not possible.

Isolation was strict. I wasn't allowed to interact with other participants or have visitors. Instead, my friends brought VHS tapes and casseroles for hospital staff to deliver directly to my room, helping break up my day by watching movies that helped ease the boredom of being stuck inside a hospital room. Though inoculated with the flu virus, my symptoms weren't nearly that intense. Although feverish symptoms appeared at times, they never manifested to any serious degree.

At around six or seven days into my flu study, I received a call in my hospital room from none other than my father. He had become extremely worried, believing my friend at the dorm had been giving false accounts each time he called. Eventually, he pressed him for the truth.

When I finally told my parents about the flu study, my father did not take it well.

"What do you mean you're in a *study*?" he shouted into the phone. "Are you sick?"

"No, Baba, I'm fine," I said quickly. "They *give* you the flu. On purpose."

There was a long pause on the line. Then: "So let me understand this. America is paying you to get sick?"

"They're not paying me to get sick," I said. "They're paying me to sit in a room and drink orange juice."

"You are selling your body for money," he declared. "If you need money, you tell me. I will sell the furniture before I let you do this."

"Please don't sell the couch," I said. "Where will you sit?" That didn't help.

Then my mother took the phone. Her voice was softer, but no less worried. "Are you really okay?" she asked. "Something terrible didn't happen that you are afraid to tell us?"

"I'm safer here than crossing the street."

She sighed. "Who volunteers to get sick?"

"Students who need grocery money," I said.

She laughed despite herself. "Next time, at least tell us before you scare your father into selling the furniture."

The whole conversation reminded me how different our worlds had become. To me, it was a strange but harmless way to make a little money. To them, it sounded like I had signed up for medical experimentation.

After eleven days, I was paid and sent home. The money helped, but what stayed with me was the reminder that before you can care for patients, it helps to know what it feels like to be one.

The University of Virginia's pre-med program was challenging and intense; every class pushed me beyond my limits in both endurance and intellect, leaving me questioning whether I had taken on too much. With its rigorous curriculum and focus on strategic planning and discipline, excelling in pre-med classes and maintaining a high GPA was not something that came easy.

One of my first challenges was managing my time efficiently. With classes including tough subjects like organic chemistry and biology, time management became crucial. To meet this need, I devised a schedule that broke up each day into manageable chunks: mornings for attending lectures and labs, afternoons spent studying, and evenings often spent in libraries burning the midnight oil—this organized approach helped me keep up with my coursework's relentless pace.

Active learning strategies quickly became my saving grace. Instead of passively reading textbooks, I engaged actively with the material by taking notes, summarizing chapters, and explaining concepts aloud. This method helped me retain information better while making studying less tedious. Forming study groups with classmates proved similarly successful: We met regularly to review material together, quiz each other on challenging topics, discuss and challenge each other as we reviewed material together, and offered different perspectives to clarify complex ideas.

Several professors and mentors helped me through all this. Dr. Garrett, my biochemistry professor, had an incredibly profound effect on me; his passion for his subject was infectious, and his teaching style was both rigorous and supportive. I spent hours in his office seeking clarification for difficult concepts or discussing potential research opportunities with him; his belief in me helped bolster my confidence and expand my interest in the sciences.

Dr. Petri was another important mentor. His approachable demeanor and willingness to assist students made him popular with students; I found his courses challenging yet engaging due to his unique way of making difficult material accessible. Beyond classroom mentoring, Dr. Petri gave me advice about my career path and how to navigate medical school applications. He also helped me get a research assistant position within his lab. Through working closely with Dr. Petri, I gained hands-on experience conducting experiments, analyzing data, presenting findings, and writing abstracts.

Balance was another integral element of my university experience. Like most students, I needed financial support while studying. I learned to juggle multiple responsibilities simultaneously while prioritizing tasks efficiently so as not to waste any of my precious time. One particularly memorable period during exam seasons, when pressure was at its height, I was pulling all-nighters, powered by caffeine and determination, in preparation for my exams. I lived at the library; my desk often became an overwhelming pile of notes and textbooks. Yet, despite our exhaustion, there was always a feeling of camaraderie among students—we all shared tips, study guides, and encouraging words with one another.

I received my first A in physical chemistry, an initially daunting subject in which I had managed to not only comprehend but excel. Working in Dr. Petri's lab, I participated in exciting projects focusing on various aspects of cellular biology. This hands-on experience proved invaluable in applying theoretical knowledge to practical situations while teaching me important life lessons such as attention to detail and critical thinking. Presenting our research at conferences was both overwhelming and exhilarating, providing me a window into scientific discovery and inquiry.

CHAPTER 14

Preparing for and navigating the Medical College Admission Test (MCAT) was one of the most challenging phases in my academic career. It was no simple task; I spent many long, late hours studying to ensure I understood every topic thoroughly. I enrolled in Kaplan prep courses for the MCAT and had virtually memorized the key topics in their materials. Mastery of the materials and the ability to process passages and arrive at conclusions through deductive reasoning were not the only tasks needed to excel. The test was timed, and this would place any speaker of English as a second language at a disadvantage. My study schedule was strictly structured with specific blocks of time dedicated to biology, chemistry, verbal reasoning, and physics sciences to maximize efficiency while using all available resources such as prep books, online courses, and study groups with peers.

One such study group met weekly to discuss challenging concepts and quiz each other on practice questions to test understanding and assess where improvement was needed. We also scheduled mock timed tests that simulated the same environment as the testing center. These sessions allowed me to gauge my progress while gauging my comprehension level as well.

Accomplishing MCAT preparation alongside my regular coursework was no small task, requiring disciplined time management. Each day, I would attend university classes, complete my assignments, and then dive straight into MCAT prep. Weekends were set aside for full-length practice tests to simulate actual exam conditions and help build the stamina required to sit through an entire exam. Although these practice tests could be exhausting, they were necessary if I wanted to do well on the main event.

The day of my MCAT test was stressful. No matter how prepared I was, it was difficult to shake the feeling of anxiety and inadequacy as I entered the testing center. Although challenging, the exam proved manageable by staying focused on what I had learned over months of study and practice. As I had suspected I would, I ran out of time. When the five-minute warning was announced, I still had several unanswered questions. These were multiple-choice formats. I ran my eyes over the remaining questions and filled in the bubbles with my number 2 pencil. When finished, however, it felt both relieving and terrifying all at once. I knew I had given it my all, but I would have to wait several weeks to see whether my efforts had paid off.

When I received my MCAT results, I saw that I had performed well above average. Even though I had run out of time during the exam, I knew I had done well enough to be considered seriously. That alone felt disorienting. In Iran, I had not been worthy of a file, let alone a future—no dossier, no transcript, no official proof that I existed academically. Here, I was being asked to present myself in painstaking detail.

The next hurdle was medical school applications. The process was lengthy and exacting: transcripts, MCAT scores, personal statements, letters of recommendation, extracurriculars, research, volunteer work—an entire paper version of a life. I was no longer invisible. I was being evaluated, measured, and considered.

Crafting the personal statement proved the hardest. I needed to communicate my commitment to medicine and to caring for others while explaining the unusual path that had brought me here. I wanted to show resilience without asking for pity, discrimination without bitterness, strength without spectacle. In a country that once refused to document me at all, I was now learning how to introduce myself—carefully, honestly—to institutions willing to listen.

My personal statement required extensive revision with feedback from mentors and peers in order to ensure it was strong enough. I asked several professors and mentors who knew me well to write letters that highlighted both my academic abilities and character; their support proved vital in strengthening my application. Dr. Petri wrote an incredible letter that showcased both my dedication to research and my potential as a physician.

The cost to apply to med school was also a significant concern and burden. The primary applications were all done through a centralized portal named AAMCAS, where each school would add an application fee. Later, the schools that had an interest in pursuing the applicant further would send secondary applications with more fees. The final stage would be the interview, if offered at all, which would involve travel and lodging costs. I reviewed the fine print with the AAMCAS application. There was a form for waiving application fees for those with financial hardship. I knew that without this form, I could only afford to apply to a handful of schools. But I also knew most of my peers had applied to over twenty-five medical schools. I opted to apply for the waiver, but worried whether schools would look down on my application because of the financial request.

Every day, I would check the mail multiple times, hoping for news. The moment when an interview invitation arrived was both relief and anxiety. In preparation for it, I thoroughly researched each school, practiced common interview questions, and considered why medicine appealed to me. I planned for everything, including my wardrobe. I used a tape measure to measure my upper and lower body and drew a diagram of what the size of my suit would be. I faxed the sketch to my parents so I could have a suit tailored for me in Iran at a much lower price than in the States. The suit arrived several weeks later, just in time for my interviews. It was an oversized olive-green suit, slightly too long in the sleeves and a shade too earnest for the moment. In a sea of black-suited, perfectly tailored medical-school hopefuls, I stood out immediately. But I didn't mind. I was there. That alone felt unreal.

For most of my life, practicing medicine had lived entirely in my imagination—something pursued in secret. Now I was walking into medical schools, shaking hands with faculty, sitting across from interviewers who asked me about my goals as if they were not only valid but expected. The interviews were nerve-wracking and exhilarating all at once. Touring campuses, meeting current students, speaking aloud about my future—it made the dream tangible in a way I hadn't allowed myself to believe was possible.

Each interview felt like a small confirmation: I belonged in these rooms. I was no longer asking for permission to dream; I was being evaluated for admission. During one conversation I connected deeply with an interviewer who shared an interest in global health. We spoke not just about medicine but also about responsibility beyond borders. As I walked out of that meeting, it struck me: I wasn't chasing an impossible future anymore. I was standing inside it.

While interviewing at Penn State in Hershey, Pennsylvania, I learned that I had listed "humor" as one of my hobbies on my application—something that immediately caught the attention of my physician interviewer. In the middle of an otherwise dry exchange, he glanced down at my file and said, "I see you're into humor. Tell me a joke!"

He paused and watched as I scrambled to recall something—anything—that would be appropriate for the moment.

"What did the agnostic man with dyslexia and insomnia do?" I asked, managing a grin.

"I don't know," he said, leaning in. "Lay it on me."

"He stayed up all night wondering if there *is* a dog."

Humor cracked the ice. We both laughed, and the tone of the interview shifted. He went on to tell me how essential humor is in human connection—and how it absolutely belongs in medicine, especially in conversations with patients.

The interview at Penn State had already taught me that unpredictability was part of this journey. After being asked to come up with a joke on the spot, I realized that every medical school encounter carried its own rhythm—sometimes awkward, sometimes revealing, always formative. My next interview was at the Virginia Commonwealth University School of Medicine in Richmond. I approached this interview with a quiet sense of urgency. I practiced mock interviews, rehearsed answers in my mind, and tried to imagine how I would present myself. The only thing I knew for certain was that I'd be wearing my olive-green suit. According to my mother, black was for mourners.

They had given me the name of my interviewer: Dr. On Topaz, a cardiologist. I repeated the name silently while sitting in the waiting area, wondering about its origin. I waited, trying to quiet the familiar mixture of hope and anxiety that accompanies moments when the future feels just within reach. The door opened, and a middle-aged man with salt-and-pepper hair stepped into the room, scanning the list in his hand. He struggled gently with the pronunciation of my name, and I recognized the effort behind the attempt. I stood quickly, almost instinctively, and met him halfway. His smile was kind, his posture welcoming, and his grip strength firm. There was no stiffness, no performative authority. Instead, there was a warmth that immediately softened the room.

Inside his office, he did something unexpected. Rather than sitting behind his desk—the invisible barrier between interviewer and applicant—he chose an armchair placed at a forty-five-degree angle from mine. He crossed his legs casually, introduced himself again, and welcomed me with a tone that felt more like a conversation than an evaluation.

"I've read your application," Dr. Topaz said. "And your personal statement."

He asked about growing up in Iran. About what it meant to belong to a minority. About discrimination. The questions felt thoughtful, not probing for weakness but searching for understanding. Eventually, he leaned forward slightly and asked, "Tell me about Baha'i."

I spoke of its central teachings—unity of humanity, the inevitability of universal peace, the emphasis on non-violence even in the face of injustice. I described the tight-knit nature of the community and the way people supported one another through hardship. As I spoke, I noticed his expression soften into a gentle smile. Then he asked a question that surprised me. "Have you ever visited the Baha'i gardens?"

His accent carried a subtle melody I could not place. I paused, wondering how he even knew about those gardens—the holy sites on Mount Carmel in Haifa, Israel, overlooking the Mediterranean Sea. I explained that I had only seen them in photographs at home, that one day I hoped to visit but had never had the resources or the chance.

He nodded, as if a memory had surfaced. "I grew up in Haifa," he said quietly. "Every day on my way to school, I passed those gardens. I remember looking up at the terraces, the golden dome shining in the sun. It was peaceful… beautiful. But I had never met anyone who was Baha'i. You're the first."

A wave of goosebumps moved through me. The improbability of that moment—an Iranian Baha'i applicant and a cardiologist from Haifa sitting face-to-face in Richmond—felt surreal.

Dr. Topaz continued, sharing that he was a descendant of Holocaust survivors. He spoke of stories from his parents, of loss and resilience, of the long shadow that discrimination casts across generations. In that room two histories intersected, two narratives shaped by exile and survival.

"I understand," he said gently. "Even though I had never met a Baha'i before… I understand."

The rest of the conversation unfolded effortlessly. We discussed my undergraduate work, my research experiences, and my aspirations in medicine. There was laughter, reflection, and a sense that this was not merely an interview but a meeting of two human beings who recognized something familiar in each other's journeys.

When our interview ended, Dr. Topaz stood, stepped forward, and gave me a warm hug. As I walked out of the building, the olive-green suit hanging imperfectly on my shoulders, I felt lighter. I did not know whether the interview would lead to an acceptance, but I carried with me a deeper reassurance: that connection and humanity could emerge in the most unlikely places. In a waiting room filled with strangers, across cultures and histories that might once have seemed irreconcilable, two people had found common ground. For a brief moment, the uncertainty of my future receded, replaced by a quiet certainty that I was not alone on this journey. Shared stories would become the next figurative passport on my journey.

Waiting anxiously for acceptance letters was a test of emotional endurance and patience. I applied to multiple institutions, each known for its particular strengths and appeal. On October 31, 1997, when I unlocked the tiny mailbox at the dormitory, it was stuffed with thick envelopes. I hurriedly removed them and examined them. One from Virginia Commonwealth University (VCU) and the other from Penn State University. I opened both of them as fast as I could muster, and I found out that I had not one but two admissions to medical schools. Even though it was nearly midnight in Iran, I called my family immediately. I didn't care about the hour—I needed them inside this moment with me. Their pride, carried across time zones and static, would make the news feel real.

When my father picked up, his voice was cautious, half-awake, braced for trouble. Who calls at midnight with good news?

For years, his words had lived in my head: *Statistics suggest you won't secure a medical school admission in the US.* He had said it to protect me, to dissuade me from leaving Iran for a dream that felt impossibly far away. Still, the sentence echoed.

Before he could ask what was wrong, I blurted out, breathless, "The statistics were wrong."

There was a pause.

"Against all odds," I continued, my voice breaking into a smile he could hear, "I'm going to be a doctor after all."

CHAPTER 15

I chose the VCU School of Medicine due to its strong focus on research and clinical training combined with its supportive environment. It was also a state school, which made tuition significantly cheaper than going out of state. My decision marked the start of an exciting new phase in my life—taking one step closer to fulfilling my dream of becoming a physician.

As I looked around the arena, I caught a wave of excitement as the sea of caps engulfed me. Atop mortarboards, tassels dangled, waiting to be flipped in matriculation. Different colors bedazzled the blanket of black gowns, signifying certain majors, paying homage to clubs or fraternities, or academic ranking. Two years too late to become officially a part of something, four of my fellow transfer students decided we would wear a color to symbolize our group, which we called The Five-Ites. We could belong just as everyone else did.

We went to Walmart and bought satin fabric in a conspicuous fuchsia color. Sewing them into sashes and ironing them to be symmetrical, The Five-Ites marched down the aisle to "Pomp and Circumstance," proudly making ourselves known to the auditorium.

For my entire life, I had been hiding my identity from a society that at every turn wanted to put a scarlet letter on my back. Now, I was doing the opposite—purposely placing an identifying mark on me and coming out of the shadows. I was no longer afraid to be seen.

My college graduation was everything my community college ceremony had not been—larger, louder, more ceremonious, draped in tradition and spectacle. Rows of caps and gowns stretched farther than I could see, the names read with practiced rhythm, the applause thunderous. I smiled and laughed with friends who had become my chosen family, exchanging knowing looks that said *we did it*—together. My aunt sat in the crowd, her presence a small but steady anchor. The moment was real, earned, unforgettable—and still, it felt unfinished without my parents there. I sent pictures of myself in my cap and gown to my parents along with news that I was going to become a homeowner during the summer before medical school.

My search began after graduation and in the outskirts of Richmond, Virginia. I hired a realtor and found a townhouse that was being offered at $75,000. It was a humble home with 1200 square feet, three bedrooms, and one-and-a-half baths. The bedrooms were upstairs; the kitchen and the living area downstairs. I figured that if I could rent out two of the smaller rooms, this would end up being cheaper than any rental. But without any income, no bank would loan me any money. I called up aunt Nahid in Maryland and asked if she could help me cosign on a loan. She had dedicated her life to the service of others, and without hesitation, she accepted. She only said, "Don't default on any mortgage payments! I have a pristine credit score, and I do not want it to be affected."

I gave her the reassurance, and before I knew it, I closed on my first home. My plan worked with minimal advertisement, I found two students from the medical school who joined me, and we all lived there very cheaply and split utilities and groceries for the next four years.

Transitioning from undergraduate to medical school was bumpy. Though I had heard numerous tales of its demands, experiencing them firsthand was altogether different; its pace was intense from day one; no gradual adjustment could be found during these initial weeks; they felt more like being dropped into the deep end of a pool.

One of the most memorable parts of my first year was attending the anatomy lab. Walking into that first lab session filled with cadavers left me both impressed and terrified; dissecting human bodies required not only technical skill but also an enduring sense of respect for those who had donated their bodies to science. Each session in the anatomy lab gave me a hands-on understanding of the human body that no textbook could ever convey. The smell of formaldehyde was strong, and the environment surreal. The cadavers were, as my professor told us, our first patients.

Adjusting to clinical skills sessions was another integral component of my first-year experience. These sessions were intended to teach us practical aspects of medicine, from taking patient histories to conducting basic physical examinations. While initially nervous about interacting with simulated patients, over time, these sessions became some of my favorites because they enabled me to apply theoretical knowledge in a practical setting and helped build my confidence for dealing with actual patients. Each session marked another step toward becoming a competent yet compassionate physician.

The sheer volume of knowledge we needed to acquire was staggering, while its pace of delivery was fast. I found myself spending long hours in libraries late into the night reviewing lecture notes, textbooks, and research papers; group study sessions often provided new insights and made learning less isolating than studying alone.

Integrating academics and a personal life was no simple task, but having a fantastic support network made a tremendous difference in terms of stress reduction. My family and friends provided incredible encouragement while being available as listening ears during difficult moments—their unfailing support kept me motivated even during tough periods.

One of the greatest joys of my first year was discovering which fields of medicine truly captivated my interest. While initially open to exploring all fields, as time progressed, certain specialties began to stand out. For example, internal medicine and cardiology caught my eye due to their complexity and potential to make significant impacts on patients' lives. Early clinical experiences like shadowing physicians or participating in patient care further cemented this interest for me; watching experienced doctors interact with patients was both inspiring and educational.

At first, there were times of self-doubt and uncertainty regarding my ability to cope with medical school demands. Managing my mental health amid constant pressure was a challenge. Medical school was intense, requiring constant exams, practicals, and recall of massive amounts of information; its high-stress environment created a risk for burnout that I still vividly recall from late nights studying in libraries with half-empty coffee cups around me and moments of doubt creeping in. There often seemed no room for error.

The physical strain was also considerable. Long hours of study and clinical rotations left little time for self-care; I struggled to maintain a healthy lifestyle, giving up sleep or meals to meet curriculum demands; this led to periods of exhaustion and physical ailments that further compounded my stress; I regularly caught colds or experienced persistent fatigue.

A new paranoia seeped in. The closer I came to graduating medical school, the more I became afraid I would be killed in a tragic accident before graduation. Ordinary activities like driving became threats to a dream I was on the cusp of realizing. I began to go out less to avoid any circumstance that would remove me from this life. That feeling of not being safe, the feeling I thought I had left behind in Iran, was back.

This was a mental health crisis I tried to combat alone. My history with people in authority, especially in an academic setting, had taught me that they were not to be trusted. Showing vulnerability in Iran was not an option in an already precarious environment. The vultures could smell fear, so I hid to avoid being their prey. Now in medical school, if I sought help for my burnout, wouldn't I risk being exposed or expelled, like I had been in Iran? Avoidance was my reliable habit, as if hiding were the answer, as it had always been. Patterns not recognized and dealt with would threaten my ability to help others. I had a choice to make. Let my coping mechanism blanket me in safety that would render me ineffective as a doctor, or face the fact that I needed help to come out of the shadows once and for all.

Had I risked leaving Iran only to forever carry the vultures inside me? My sacrifices and those of the people supporting me would be all for naught. I found the nerve to knock on the door of a university counselor. For the first time, I shared my inner thoughts and processed the trauma I had endured: the oppression, the war, the fear, the smuggling, the assimilation. Before that moment, I hadn't considered the gravitas of it all. Acquainting myself with my repressed emotions became my passport to a freedom of authenticity that made me feel like an American.

The medical school demands also created a considerable financial strain. Without health insurance and minimal financial support from family, managing medical expenses was often an uphill struggle without adequate coverage. I recall the anxiety of not having health coverage, fearing an accident might happen. The school required that we maintain health insurance upon matriculation. But after the first year, they no longer asked for evidence of coverage. So, to save money, I went without health insurance the last three years of medical school. This also meant that I was always afraid to visit the student health center or to seek therapy when I felt down. Lucky for me, my sister Shahrzad would soon join me in America.

When I left Iran in 1994 after a year of studies at BIHE, she had already completed three years at the BIHE studying pharmacological sciences. Given her academic aptitude and superior performance in high school, if Shahrzad had been granted access to university studies in Iran, she would have secured admission in any specialty of her choice at any university.

In 1994, Bahá'ís were categorically denied Iranian passports. But by 1999, the Islamic Republic had silently abandoned the practice of withholding passports from Iranian Bahá'ís, and my sister was able to secure a passport. By this time, she had already graduated with her bachelor's degree equivalent from the BIHE and was newly married—a wedding that I sadly did not have the privilege to attend.

Once my sister received her Iranian passport, she too—also an American citizen by birth—was finally able to leave Iran. She came straight to my home in Richmond, Virginia, where I was in my second year of medical school. Seeing her again after five years apart felt like the closing of a wide loop. We were no longer children shaped by scarcity and rivalry, but two adults rediscovering the bond that had always held us, now facing the practical realities of rebuilding a life.

She was older than me by two years, but this time, I had experience to share with her instead of the other way around. I had been carried—by teachers, neighbors, smugglers, diplomats, and strangers who had become family. Now it was my turn to become part of that chain for her. Together, we navigated hurdles that felt painfully familiar: graduate schools unwilling to recognize a BIHE degree and applications returned with polite rejections. I worked side by side with her on personal statements, GRE preparation, interviews—doing for her what others had done for me.

Some doors remained closed. But a few opened. Temple University saw what Iran refused to: promise. My sister was admitted to their pharmaceutics PhD program with full funding, her tuition waived. Soon after, her husband was granted US residency and immigrated.

My sister and her husband, both now holding doctorates from American universities, are living proof of what is lost when talent is suppressed and what is gained when it is welcomed. Iran's loss became America's gain once more—not because of luck, but because someone, somewhere, chose to open a door and pass the passport along.

* * *

I was a third-year medical student on my surgery rotation when the world shook on September 11, 2001. We were already scrubbed in when the circulating nurse glanced at her computer monitor and froze. "Something's happening in New York," she said quietly, almost to herself.

No one looked up at first. In an operating room, alarms are constant, rumors meaningless. We kept working. A few minutes later, the charge nurse stepped through the doors, her face pale.

"There's been an attack," she said. "In New York."

An *attack* was still vague enough to feel accidental—an explosion, a fire, a mistake. But when word spread that a second plane had hit, the tone changed. This was no accident. This was something else. But what?

By the time we closed and de-scrubbed, every television in the hospital was on. Staff crowded into lounges, hallways, anywhere there was a screen. We watched the towers burn, then collapse—steel folding like paper. Someone whispered, "How many people were inside?" No one answered.

Then came the news that the Pentagon had been hit. Richmond wasn't New York—but Washington was close. Ninety miles. Close enough. The hospital went on diversion. All elective surgeries were canceled. Operating rooms were cleared and held open, waiting. Hospitals don't do that lightly. That's what you do when you expect mass casualties. I felt something old rise inside me. This wasn't just news. This was trauma—national trauma. War, unfolding in real time. I had come to America to escape that word, and here it was again, standing in the room with me.

My mind shifted into clinical mode. *What will we see? Burns? Inhalation injuries? Crush trauma? How many? How do we triage?*

I gave myself a silent pep talk: *You know how to do this. You can start IVs. You can transfuse blood. You can assist. You can hold retractors. If they come, you will rise to the occasion.*

I was terrified. I was wired with adrenaline. But beneath it all was duty. Even as a student, I knew I was meant to show up. As we watched the ongoing pictures of downtown Manhattan, Pennsylvania, and DC, I thought of the Iran–Iraq war. Of hiding in stairwells. Of the sonic booms that rattled our teeth. Of the neighbor upstairs who would collapse into panic every time the ground shook, sobbing uncontrollably while my father tried to calm her.

"We're alive," he would repeat, over and over, like a spell. Now, decades later, I wondered about the people who weren't alive. The ones trapped. The ones burning. The ones running toward the smoke instead of away from it.

For days afterward, the country moved differently. People were gentler. Strangers smiled in elevators. They asked how you were and waited for the answer. It reminded me of my childhood community—the Bahá'í community—and how pressure and fear had made us tighter, kinder, more attentive to one another. I remember thinking: *Why does it take catastrophe for us to remember how to be human?*

A few weeks later, studying in the dental school library—it was quieter, newer, and better lit—I spotted a group of Saudi dental students gathered around a table. We'd crossed paths before. There was the familiar nod—minority recognition.

One of them smiled and waved me over. "Brother Nizam," he said. "Come sit."

I hesitated, then joined them. After a moment, one of them leaned back and said casually,

"It was America's turn to suffer."

I stared at him.

"For what?" I asked.

"For imperialism. For Israel," another added. "They've killed enough."

These weren't uneducated people. These were top students, sponsored by their government, receiving elite training in the United States. Beneficiaries of the very system they now condemned. I felt something snap into place.

"I don't believe killing innocent people is ever justified," I said. "Not anywhere. Not for any reason."

They pushed back. They spoke of deserved pain. Of balance. Of pride. And suddenly I was seven years old again, standing in a schoolyard while being forced to chant "Death to America," reciting words of hatred I didn't believe as proof of my belonging. I had risked my life to escape that ideology. And here it was finding me again, assuming I was part of its tribe because of my name, my face, my geography. I stood up.

"This is hate speech," I said. "Firefighters are digging through ash with their bare hands. Families are waiting for bodies that will never be found. And you're celebrating?"

Silence.

I walked away knowing that extremism doesn't belong to one country. It migrates. It adapts. And it counts on silence. I had spent my life learning when to be quiet to survive. Those days were over. I didn't know then that the antidote to that silence wouldn't be confrontation but *care* and that I would find my voice not in arguments, but at the bedside.

As a third-year student, when I rotated through pediatrics, I often found myself thinking of my mother. The way she leaned in and listened. The way she never rushed a frightened parent, even when the night was long and her living room full. On the oncology floor, I watched children face diagnoses that would terrify any adult. Some were terminal. Yet, what stayed with me was not despair but the steadiness of their parents—hovering over beds, clinging to each scan, each lab result, each whispered hope of a miracle. In those hallways, life was treated as sacred, no matter how small or fragile.

I could not help but contrast this with the stories I had grown up hearing in Iran—of children sent into minefields to clear paths for soldiers, their small bodies reduced to strategy. The difference was not just political. It was philosophical. Here, every life mattered. There, life was expendable.

On pulmonary service, I cared for children with sickle cell disease and cystic fibrosis—small for their age, chronically ill, yet astonishingly joyful. One moment pierced me deeply: Many of the children couldn't pronounce cystic fibrosis. Instead, they said, "I have sixty-five roses."

The innocence of it broke my heart. It reminded me why medicine exists: not just to extend life but to protect hope. Years later, when Islamic Republic forces stormed hospitals and arrested doctors for treating injured protesters, the contrast became even sharper. In America, the doctor–patient relationship is sacred. In Iran, even that sanctuary can be violated. I realized then that choosing medicine was also choosing a moral stance: Care must never be conditional.

That question followed me quietly through training. *What if one day I were asked to care for someone who represented everything that had harmed my family? Could I still honor the oath I had taken?* I had been trained to value life—*all* life. Even if an agent of the Islamic Republic were to be under my care, I would never compromise my oath. I would never refuse care. I would never stoop to his level to discriminate.

One afternoon, I was in pre-op. The anesthesiologist mentioned that the patient spoke Persian—originally from Afghanistan—and thought I might help. Afghans speak Dari, a dialect close enough to Persian to allow real communication. When I introduced myself in her language, her face softened instantly. In a room filled with machines and strangers, recognition mattered. She was scheduled for a cesarean section—her fifth—but this time it was different. She had placenta increta, a life-threatening condition that would require an immediate hysterectomy to prevent catastrophic bleeding. I translated carefully. Step by step. The risks. The blood loss. The surgery. The possibility of death.

When I finished, she stared at me—not panicked, but frozen. I gently asked if my Persian was difficult to understand. "No," she said quietly. "I only have three years of schooling. The words are hard."

Then she told me her story. The Taliban had ended her education. She had been married as a child. She had dreamed of more. Her questions weren't about survival. They were about dignity.

"If you remove my uterus," she asked, "can I still be intimate with my husband? Does he need to know? Will the blood for my transfusion be from a Muslim?"

She never asked if she might die. Her surgery was difficult. She bled heavily. She needed multiple transfusions. But she survived. The baby was healthy. When we spoke to her husband afterward, he asked only one question: "How is the baby?" He wasn't even at his wife's bedside.

In some cultures, the surgeon later explained, a woman without a uterus is no longer considered whole. That was what she feared—not death, but erasure. I thought of Iran. Of women whose worth is measured narrowly. Of lives shaped by forces that deny education, agency, and choice. Of how lucky I had been to not be erased. It taught me that compassion must go beyond clinical care—that true healing begins with understanding where someone comes from, not just what illness they carry.

I was tested on this very lesson soon after when the trauma alert came through the beeper just after midnight. Gunshot wound. Hemodynamically unstable. Massive blood loss. We moved on instinct. Down the hall, into the trauma bay, where scissors made quick work of the patient's clothes—fabric peeled away to expose the body to light, hands, urgency. His blood pressure was barely holding. His pulse thin and erratic. We had seconds.

And then I saw the tattoos. A large KKK emblem on his right chest. A swastika on the left. A chain inked across his torso, broken in the middle—the kind of symbol you see on men who've known prison, rage, allegiance to the devil.

We moved him straight to the operating room.

His spleen was ruptured. Blood pooled fast. We activated the massive transfusion protocol—unit after unit of red cells, plasma, platelets, cryoprecipitate. I managed lines, blood gases, pressure, and fluids. At one point, I looked around the room. The surgeon was Jewish.

The scrub tech was a Black woman. The nurse was Filipino. I was Persian. Others moved in and out—Hispanic, Asian, accents layered like bricks. Every one of us was someone this man, by his ink alone, would likely reject.

But there we were—doing everything possible to save his life. The irony sat heavy. This man's body declared allegiance to white supremacy, to exclusion, to hatred of people who looked like us. And still, we fought for him. We gave him blood donated by strangers of every race and belief, given without knowing whose life it would save. He survived. Days later, after he was extubated and transferred out of the ICU, I went to see him. I introduced myself. Told him I had been part of the team that kept him alive. He took my hand in both of his. Held it tightly. Thanked me. His eyes filled. He was gentle. Grateful. Disarmingly kind.

I left that room unsettled. I had judged him by what was written on his skin. I had assumed who he was, what he believed, what he would think of me. Maybe those tattoos still meant exactly what I thought they did. Maybe they didn't. I would never ask. It wasn't relevant.

Years before I took the Hippocratic Oath, I was taught its spirit. In anatomy lab, our first instructor said it plainly: "This body was donated by a person who trusted you. Treat it with respect. This is your first patient."

There would be no jokes. No desecration. No forgetting that someone once lived inside this body. I had gratitude for the cadaver, which was the first dead body I had ever seen. It stood in stark contrast to my earliest memories of death. As a child in Iran, during the Iran–Iraq War, my middle school announced that one of its former students had become a martyr. A casket was brought into the schoolyard, draped in the Iranian flag. We were lined up and instructed to pass it hand to hand. Children. Touching a coffin. Teachers weeping. Quranic verses blaring.

I remember feeling confused—*disturbed*—certain that death was being staged, planted deliberately into our young lives to serve an ideology. In medicine, death is never propaganda. It is treated with gravity, humility, and restraint. Standing in that operating room years later—saving a man whose beliefs may have despised my very existence—I understood that medicine is a sanctuary from ideology. Once you step into that role, there is a sanctity you don't compromise. You don't choose who deserves care. You don't ask what they stand for. You don't weigh their past against their pulse. You save the life in front of you.

Like these moments, some in medicine arrive quietly but change you for good. One of mine happened not in a hospital, but on Marshall Street in Richmond, where food trucks lined the sidewalk outside our rotations. There was an older woman who ran one of them. She remembered my name, asked about my studies, and sent me off with encouragement that felt almost maternal. On days I didn't have cash, she would wave it off—"Pay me tomorrow." It echoed something I had known before, when my father and a kabob shop owner would gently insist the same, as if dignity could be preserved through quiet generosity. For $5.50, she offered more than food—she offered kindness in the middle of unforgiving training.

Then one day, I was assigned to evaluate a patient presenting with suicidal ideation. It was a routine task, one we approached with clinical structure and emotional caution. I glanced at the name on the chart without recognition and walked into the room prepared for another difficult, but not unfamiliar, encounter. The smell of alcohol was immediate and overwhelming. And then I saw her. It was the same woman.

She looked at me, and even through her intoxication, recognition flickered instantly across her face. A faint, fragile smile appeared—the same smile that had greeted me so many times on Marshall Street, now dimmed. I knelt beside her bed, trying to hide my disbelief and took her hands in mine. In that moment, the roles we had quietly occupied in each other's lives were laid bare in a way neither of us had anticipated.

Her story unfolded slowly, painfully. There was abuse at home. There was fear. There was poverty. She showed me scars. Bruises that had not yet faded. And beneath it all was a profound exhaustion, a sense that the life she was living had become unbearable. She told me she no longer wanted to continue. As she spoke, tears came to both of us—not the restrained, clinical tears of professionalism, but the unguarded kind that emerge when two human beings meet each other without pretense.

In that room, I was confronted with a truth that no textbook had ever adequately conveyed: how little we often know about the lives unfolding around us. Here was a woman who had, in her own quiet way, supported me—fed me, encouraged me, believed in my future—while carrying a burden I had never once paused to imagine. I had accepted her kindness without ever asking what it cost her to give it. That day emphasized a principle we are taught in medicine but do not fully understand until we experience it: never assume, never judge, and never reduce a person to the fragment of themselves you happen to see. Every patient, every passerby, every familiar face carries a story that is often invisible—and sometimes unbearable.

In Virginia, I noticed how families flock to hospitals when a loved one is having surgery. Entire clans filled pre-op areas—grandparents, aunts, siblings—everyone present to witness and worry together. During a routine pediatric surgery, we invited a grandmother to accompany her toddler into the induction room. The intention was kindness—to soften the moment with compassion and empathy. She held the baby as I delivered the anesthetic through a mask. But when the child drifted into anesthesia, his breathing changed and his eyes rolled back. To me, it was routine. To her, it was terror. She bolted—baby in her arms—out of the hospital. I chased her into the parking lot, shouting, trying to reach her so I could keep the baby's airway open, knowing how dangerous that moment was to have a partially anesthetized baby with no monitors attached and in the arms of the panicked grandmother. Finally, I caught up to her, pulled the baby away, and ran back to the operating room. I stabilized the child. The surgery went smoothly. No harm done. But the lesson lingered: Even compassion requires boundaries. Good intentions are not always enough. In medicine, timing, clarity, and vigilance save lives.

Across these moments—oncology wards, operating rooms, whispered translations—I kept seeing the same thing I had seen growing up in Iran and at BIHE: people doing the best they could with what they were given. My mother had done it in a makeshift clinic. BIHE teachers had done it in living rooms. Doctors here did it in hospitals protected by law. Different countries. Same calling.

Medicine became, for me, another passport—not out of a country, but into people's lives. A way to honor the value of every human being, especially those whose dignity has been denied. And in that sense, the journey that began with a hidden passport had always been leading here.

CHAPTER 16

Unlike my community college and University of Virginia graduations, where no family members were able to attend due to being denied passports, all my family was with me for medical school graduation. Iran had finally begun to loosen its laws, and my parents were granted passports for the first time since their original ones were revoked after the Revolution of 1979. My Hippocratic oath marked a tearful family reunion of the important people who played major parts in each leg of my journey. Aunts and uncles had been the soft landing during a hard transition from Iran to Europe to Maryland. My mother was able to hug her siblings after decades of separation, and unknown first cousins from as far away as California paused their busy lives to celebrate a new doctor in the family. America had made us a family again.

We had achieved the ultimate workaround. My mother had been my rock throughout my education; having her there to witness this milestone meant everything to me. My parents themselves had become unwilling educators, co-founding BIHE, so to see them in the presence of those people who had believed in their son, who had taken a chance on me was like my own personal version of Mosaic House, my two worlds finally becoming one.

Held in a grand auditorium, the atmosphere was electric—an exhilarating combination of excitement, relief, and hopefulness for the future. The acoustics were as crisp as the air between the valleys of the trails where I used to hike with my friends. The same feeling of expansiveness lifted me. Within the buzz of the grand venue, I was now catching echoes of a voice I had fought hard to find.

One by one, our names were called as we made our way across the stage to receive diplomas. When mine came up, I felt overwhelmed with emotion as this piece of paper represented not just years of hard work on my part but also sacrifices made by my family who believed so strongly in me. This diploma was the ultimate passport, descending from three literal passports, all traded in for one medical degree. I was not only free; I had the power to build a prosperous life for a future family of my own.

Being a physician herself, my mother was the one to hood me, an age-old tradition with deep symbolic significance. As she placed the hood over my shoulders, her eyes wide and wet, my mother whispered, "I told you you'd make it."

The audience around us became the blurry backdrop of a vivid moment in which only my mother and I existed. I leaned in until my lips touched her ears. "No, Maman. Don't you remember, we were together in this. *We* made it."

My medical school diploma was the last passport I would ever need. I finally would be able to claim the future my parents had guarded for me, and I had dreamed of as a child. When Halley's Comet travels back, I won't be wishing. I'll be telling her how far I went—and why it was worth it.

EPILOGUE

After years of lectures, exams, and long nights that blurred into one another, the finish line was crossed. I had spent so much time focused on getting there—on proving that I could—that I rarely paused to consider what came next. I believed, perhaps naively, that the hardest part was behind me. That once I wore that hood, the path would become clearer, steadier, and more certain. But that is not doctoring.

I trained in anesthesiology at the University of Virginia, where years of discipline, resilience, and perseverance culminated in board certification. From there, I moved west to Arizona, choosing to work in a hospital that cared for the most vulnerable.

At Maricopa Medical Center, I treated patients from every walk of life: immigrants navigating unfamiliar systems, families burdened by illness and circumstance, and individuals whose language or legal status had kept them from seeking care until they could no longer endure the pain. I cared for newborns with congenital defects and children injured by trauma no child should ever experience. I held hands with grieving parents. I cared for African women in labor whose bodies bore the lasting scars of female genital mutilation. I treated undocumented patients who had avoided doctors for years out of fear, arriving only when illness made hiding impossible. I cared for laborers with catastrophic burns and with no family to claim them. In those moments, medicine became more than science—it became trust, compassion, and dignity restored, in keeping with the oath I took on graduation day.

I also spent time at a cancer hospital where I cared for a patient whose primary disease had been brought under control, but who carried a few metastatic lesions in his lung. The decision was made to proceed with surgical resection, an effort to reduce tumor burden and extend life. The operation began thoracoscopically, with careful placement of cameras into the chest. But prior radiation had rendered the tissues fragile, almost unforgiving. After hours of effort, the surgeon made the difficult but necessary decision to convert to an open thoracotomy.

What followed unfolded with the kind of suddenness that leaves no time for only action. A tear in the pulmonary artery. Tissue too friable to hold sutures. Blood loss that escalated in moments. We activated massive transfusion protocols, worked in the constraints of lateral positioning, and fought physiology as it slipped away from us. Chest compressions were ineffective in that position; we asked for open cardiac massage while the surgeon, with extraordinary focus, tried to achieve hemostasis. Despite everything we lost him on the table.

There are moments in medicine that do not end when the case ends. They follow you. They live in your body, as this one does for me. One of the hardest parts was not the resuscitation itself, but walking into a quiet consultation room where a family had been waiting for hours, holding onto hope. Standing beside the surgeon, I felt the weight of words that no one ever wants to say. In that moment, there is no algorithm, no guideline—only grief, shared in a space where time seems to stop.

For a long time after, I carried that day with me in ways I did not fully understand. They just don't prepare young med students for a time like this. You think being a doctor is about saving lives…until you are inevitably humbled.

Each time I returned to that hospital, my body would react before my mind could catch up. Driving into the parking lot, walking those familiar halls, I felt it physically. A tightening, a heaviness, an echo of something unresolved. It was a reminder that even when we are trained to compartmentalize, the human within the physician does not disappear. And if it ever does, it's a signal to abandon the white coat.

The most difficult lesson medicine has taught me is that there are limits to what we can control. I came to understand this lesson more deeply, not in the operating room, but at home.

My mother, who had been a physician, a teacher, a light in so many lives, spent her final days battling metastatic breast cancer under hospice care in my home. I sat by her bedside for hours, not as a doctor, but as a son. I watched the quiet progression of dying—the subtle shifts, the slowing rhythms, the transition into a space where medicine no longer intervenes, but simply bears witness.

There was nothing to fix. No protocol to initiate. No intervention to reverse the course. It was painful and humbling. And that was, in many ways, the most profound and painful realization of all. I watched her, day by day, as if a flower were gently surrendering its petals. The woman who had been a pillar of strength, a source of wisdom, a presence that filled every room, gradually receded into stillness. Until one day, she took her final breath.

That evening, I stood there in a quiet disbelief that no amount of training, no number of years in medicine, could have altered that moment. The person I loved most in the world was beyond my reach—not because I had failed, but because it was simply her time.

Medicine had taught me how to fight for life. My mother taught me how to accept its limits. If there is a quiet truth that emerges from these experiences, it is that our role is not always to save, but to serve. Not always to cure, but to care. Not always to control outcomes, but to meet each moment with presence, compassion, and humility. In the end, what we offer—whether in an operating room or at a bedside—is not perfection. It is ourselves.

In my grief, medicine continued to ask something of me. So not in spite of loss, but alongside it, I returned to the work, carrying forward both what I had been taught and what I had lived.

When many believed the anesthesia market in Phoenix was already saturated, I co-founded Grand Canyon Anesthesia with a colleague. What others saw as too risky, we approached with vision, discipline, and relentless work. Over time, the practice grew, eventually leading to a successful transaction with a private equity firm that few imagined possible in less than a decade.

Alongside clinical work, I remained committed to education, holding faculty positions at the University of Arizona and Midwestern University, helping train and mentor future physicians. Teaching reminded me that knowledge, once denied to me, was now something I could freely give.

With achievement came a deeper understanding of responsibility—not as obligation, but as privilege. The privilege of serving, opening doors for others, and lifting people forward. This belief was inherited from my parents, especially my late mother, whose quiet devotion to healing and teaching shaped my understanding of service, and from my father, whose integrity and foresight gave me the gift of choice long before I understood its value.

That same belief led me to found the Simpatico Foundation, a nonprofit dedicated to bringing people together through the arts and shared humanity. It later led me to serve on the board of the Iran Human Rights Documentation Center, continuing a lifelong commitment to bearing witness and giving voice to those silenced.

Through medicine, education, philanthropy, and advocacy, the boy who once fled repression built a life centered on service. But this story is not mine alone. It belongs to the teachers who opened doors. To the mentors who believed. To the communities that welcomed a stranger. To the countless hands that carried me forward. To the many human passports that opened impossible doors. This book is proof that adversity, when met with courage and faith, can give rise to extraordinary possibility, and that success, if it means anything at all, must be shared. *Passport to Freedom* is, at its heart, an American story—not forged in ease, but in struggle; not in isolation, but in community.

ACKNOWLEDGMENTS

My deepest thanks to my agent, Adam Chromy of Movable Type Management—the ultimate advocate. Adam not only found the right publishing home for this book, but brought with him a rare commitment to storytelling that truly impacts the reader. His guidance—both editorial and strategic—helped shape this memoir into what it has become. He saw not just what the story was, but what it could be.

To Michele Matrisciani, a talented writer in her own right, thank you for stepping in as both creative partner and my steady guide. You supported me in every aspect of the writing process, then seamlessly shifted into the role of strategist, walking me through the many esoteric details of publishing. You listened deeply, found themes and connections I hadn't noticed, and helped bring coherence and clarity to a lifetime of experiences. You made this journey not only possible, but rewarding and fun.

To Gretchen Young and Regalo Press, thank you for creating a platform where voices like mine can rise and expand the world around us, and for seeing the value in my story. Your company's mission to support philanthropy and deep support of nonprofit organizations set Regalo apart in this space, and it was a true pleasure to work with you.

To the entire team at Regalo Press and Post Hill Press—thank you for your care, precision, and collaboration. Caitlin Burdette, thank you for keeping the process moving with clarity and calm. DJ Schuette, your thoughtful copyediting and constant encouragement made the manuscript stronger at every turn. And to the designer who brought this cover to life—thank you for your creativity, your openness to feedback, and for making me feel like a true partner in the process.

Writing a book, I've come to realize, is not unlike practicing medicine. No meaningful outcome is achieved alone. It takes a team—each person bringing their expertise, their perspective, their steady hands—to guide something fragile into its fullest form.

With gratitude to all of you.

ABOUT THE AUTHOR

Nizam Missaghi, M.D., is an Iranian-American physician. He left his native Iran after the completion of high school due to being deprived of access to higher education as a religious minority in the Islamic Republic.

He completed his undergraduate studies at the University of Virginia and pursued his medical education at Virginia Commonwealth University School of Medicine. After completion of his residency in anesthesiology, he moved to the Phoenix metro area, where he is a founding member of Grand Canyon Anesthesia and a clinical assistant professor of anesthesiology at the University of Arizona School of Medicine and Midwestern University.

He currently serves as the chairman of the board for Iran Human Rights Documentation Center, where human rights abuses in the Islamic Republic are investigated, verified, and documented. He is the author of multiple articles in Persian and English that focus on human rights and Iran-related matters. He has given multiple presentations about social psychology and human behavior. He is also the founder of The Simpatico Foundation, a nonprofit organization headquartered in Arizona that promotes diversity and the arts